Making Choices:
Aligning Strategic Business Execution with Strategy Through Project Portfolio Management

Dr. Te Wu

Brian Williamson

iExperi Press ▪ Montclair, NJ

Aligning Strategic Business Execution with Strategy Through Project Portfolio Management

Authors: Te Wu, Brian Williamson
Contributors: Chelsey Pienaar, Bob Grieser
Publisher: iExperi Press

Published in the United States
ISBN-13: 978-1-941913-08-6

Version 1.1
Printed by iExperi Press using CreateSpace, a DBA of On-Demand Publishing LLC

DEDICATION

This book is dedicated to all the portfolio management professionals who confront the challenges of not only doing the right things but also messiness getting the right things done.

About the Authors

Prof. Dr. Te Wu is the founder and CEO of PMO Advisory LLC, a management consulting firm specializing in strategic business execution and a PMI Global Registered Education Provider providing training in portfolio, program, project, agile, and risk management and project management office (PMO). Te has more than 20 years of experience in management consulting, having worked with industry leaders such as KPMG, Accenture, Oracle, Kraft, Standard and Poor's, Chase Bank, Corning Incorporated, and LexisNexis. He is an expert at implementing transformative change, enterprise resource planning (ERP), master data management (MDM), data analysis, and process optimization and simulation.

For the past 15 years, Te has also held professorships at multiple universities in New Jersey and New York teaching international business, general management, organizational change, and project management. These include Stevens Institute of Technology, Touro Graduate School of Business, and Montclair State University. Te is one of an estimated 200 professionals worldwide certified in Portfolio (PfMP®), Program (PgMP®), Project (PMP®), Risk (PMI-RMP®) Management, and ITIL Foundation. In his spare time, he is working on a range of publications and research.

In addition, Te serves as a board member and in various advisory capacities for multiple educational institutions. Te is an avid volunteer with Project Management Institute where he serves on the core committees for portfolio and risk management. He is also a voting member of the U.S. Technical Advisory Team (US TAG) 258 for Project, Program, and Portfolio representing United States in the corresponding committee of the International Standard Organization.

Mr. Brian Williamson is a strategic portfolio, program, and project management executive, with over 22 years of experience managing and implementing large-scale enterprise software applications. He has extensive experience in the micro verticals of finance, supply chain, and human capital management spanning several industry verticals. Over the course of his career, he has been very fortunate to have worked with a number of industry leaders including Praxair; Western Connecticut Health Network; Avaap; PMO Advisory; several Big 4 Strategic Advisory firms; Oracle; and Infor to name just a few. He is an expert in business analysis, requirements management, strategic planning, leading transformational change, and helping organizations align their portfolios with their mission, vision, goals, and objectives.

At the time of this publishing, Brian is counted among the less than 20 people globally to hold all the renewable certifications from the Project Management Institute: Portfolio (PfMP®), Program (PgMP®), Project (PMP®), Business Analysis (PMI-PBA ®), Risk (PMI-RMP®), Scheduling (PMI-SP®), and Agile (PMI-ACP®). Brian also holds the designation of ITIL® Expert in IT Service Management, having earned the following credentials from Axelos: Foundation in IT Service Management (v2011), Release Control and Validation (RCV), Service Offerings and Agreements (SOA), Operational Support and Analysis (OSA), Service Operation (SO), and Managing Across the Lifecycle (MALC). He is also a Certified Fraud Examiner (CFE) by the Association of Certified Fraud Examiners and has received extensive training in Six Sigma.

As a consultant, trainer, and coach, Brian has mentored and educated dozens of C-Level Executives, Senior Level Practitioners, and industry professionals on the theory, strategic execution, and tools & techniques related to Portfolio and Program Management.

Preface

We created this book as an experiment to enhance the learning of complex, experienced-based subjects such as portfolio management. As executives and trainers, the authors realize the limitation of traditional training resources. In most cases and for most people, the knowledge retention is low for one or more of the following reasons:

1. Most textbooks often simplify and idealize scenarios. In real business, conditions are far more complex.
2. Many textbooks, lectures, and presentations are rather boring. It is often a struggle to stay engaged.
3. Even when the classes and readings are exciting, they can be difficult to synthesize.

To enhance learning, this book borrows a technique from our ancestors at a time before the written words became popular. Then, the primary vehicle for knowledge sharing and retention is through stories. By highlight selective firestorms through the life of the protagonist (Isabella Garcia), readers can be witnesses of the challenges that she faced and how she went about solving them.

As a work of fiction, the authors understood that we trivialized some situations and liberally minimized or exaggerated some points to make the story more lively. Nonetheless, all the firestorms are real as they are based on the authors' experiences.

So sit back and enjoy the book. We also love to hear from you, so please register the book and provide your feedback: www.pmoadvisory.com/product-registration/.

Table of Contents

Chapter 1: Questioning Success - Great Tool, Little Value

A loud siren suddenly hits my ears like a violin; it's another fire drill for the office building. I had really hoped to be out of the office by now. I've been subjected to one too many of these over the past week. Why can't they just get it right? Anyway, I guess it's important. And it's not like I was doing anything constructive. I'd been staring at the same report for the past, well, I don't even know how many minutes. And I *still* have no idea how to solve this knowledge management issue.

I grab my handbag from my desk and follow the sluggish crowds through the fire exit at a pace that says their lives are not exactly in danger. At this rate, it looks like we'll be having another one of these tomorrow. I think some of the others have noticed me shaking my head. I barely see them. I can't help thinking that I've done *everything* right to turn this project around. When I accepted the offer to head up a new Strategic Project Management Office (SPMO), the Knowledge Management Project (KMP) already had a series of obstacles. It was tracking behind schedule and over budget. It had been clearly underestimated from its very inception. Fortunately, with the support of our Sponsor, Alexandra Harris, we managed to convince the Governance Committee to nearly double the project budget and schedule. The project has remained on track ever since and has been running favorable to plan. I mean, nobody can deny it's been a scheduling and budgeting success. Alex agreed that we've achieved our scope. The main focus of the project was the delivery of the knowledge management information technology application, and that's what we've done. We've successfully created a knowledge management information system. With the project running favorably, we were even able to get the budget to accommodate the necessary staff training across the company; which took some fighting effort I might add. And I really believe that the project team itself has confidence in the relevance and practicality of the system. Yet, after six months post go-live, we sit with a creeping problem that is now highly visible. The knowledge management system is simply not being used. If it's not being used, then we're failing to leverage two of the organization's most valuable assets, our people' knowledge, and their ability to collaborate and share this knowledge. And the collection, connection and utilization of these assets could go a long way toward reaching our strategic objectives. I let out a long sigh. All that hard work with little value for the organization. No! I need to fix this.

The next morning I wake up with a headache. Probable diagnosis? A restless night, wondering how I'm going to explain the disappointing results of a great system to the Governance Committee; and maybe even our company President, Bob Simmons. After all, it *is* a great system. What a conundrum this has become. I think it's time to get some other heads in the game. Mine hurts.

I get up and get coffee on the go. It's early, but Rick's already getting the kids dressed for school. I open my laptop and start typing an email to Adena Nazari and Scott Rogers. I want to meet with them both today. Who better to give perspective than Nazari and Scott? After all, Nazari is the Senior Project Manager on the KMP, and Scott's headed up the team responsible for designing and building the knowledge management technology. We all have busy schedules, but I've managed to set the meeting for 2pm.

It feels like an eternity as the clock ticks closer to our meeting time. I stare impatiently at my screen, waiting for the meeting reminder to pop up on my Google calendar. I have plenty of problems to solve, of course, but this one is bothering me most. Scott is the first to knock on my door, and he's excited. He's come up with a variety of system enhancements to improve the location of knowledge sources. He's in the middle of losing me in the technicalities of his idea when Nazari walks in. Polite banter and a few laughs start the conversation, then I dive straight into my dilemma. "Thanks for making the time to meet today, guys. I've requested this meeting because I'd like to chat with you both about the Knowledge Management Project, and I suspect that your closeness to the project will be valuable", I began. "Would you both agree that the knowledge management system, from a project perspective, has been a success?" Definitely, they both agree. "We've quite literally met every target for development in the revised schedule," says Scott. "Okay," I say, "so we're all in agreement. But, while the project targets were met, we haven't *actually* seen any effect in the company." They both seem a little confused. So I decide to be more specific. "Scott, that report you sent me yesterday, it's a bleak picture." He nods grimly. "Talented team members have invested paid time into a system that's not being used by the rest of the staff. There's been little to no observable increase in collaboration, documenting of processes, efficiencies or anything else for that matter. So far it appears as though we've wasted precious resources on this project". "So, my question is *why*?"

Neither of them needs much time before they've come up with an answer. Nazari jumps in first with a suggestion that staff needs more training on how to use the knowledge management system. "The system is new to them, and some people are not good at this type of thing. Maybe we should find out who would like additional training?" Scott looks irritated at this comment. "Are you kidding, Nazari? The training was top notch. "My team put a huge amount of time into designing and delivering that training. I've heard no complaints from anyone. In fact, *you* even reviewed the training and gave the thumbs up." Nazari is a gentle character by nature; unusual for someone in his position. But he's got this knack of getting people to perform, simply because they like and respect him. "I really didn't mean it that way" said Nazari, humbly. "I just meant that maybe we've assumed that *everyone* understands how to use the system, when in reality there may be a few who need a little extra attention when it comes to technology." Scott isn't giving in easily. "The system is completely intuitive and extremely user-friendly. How could anyone possibly need anything more than the comprehensive training we already gave them?"

I sense it's time for me to interrupt. "Okay, I get your point Nazari. But even if you're right, even if there *are* a few who haven't grasped the excellent training that Scott's team put together, *some* are simply not enough to produce the dismal results that we're seeing. Scott grins with affirmation. Noticing this, I decide to shift the spotlight. "Scott, do you have any better ideas? We need answers guys". "Sure I do," says Scott. "I already shared some of my ideas for improving the system. Maybe the knowledge management system itself is the problem. Maybe we need a few more system enhancements before we can achieve the results you're looking for?"

After a little more back and forth we decided that it's worth exploring both avenues. After all, there needs to be *some* explanation to the Governance Committee as to why this investment is not paying off. Knowing Bob, he'll want some answers too. Especially after I motivated for the budget to be doubled - and then spent it. A perfect example of the pressures of reporting to the President of the company. I have my next check-in with him on Monday. I'd like to go prepared to admit the faults, but also to offer informed solutions. But before we know 'how' to change, we need to understand 'what' to change. And the best place to start is with the obstacle itself; the people. We need to hear from them why they haven't been using the system.

Some further discussion leads us to the next step, which is to survey the company staff. Scott, Nazari and I get started immediately. Most of the questions center around the training. "Was the training sufficient?" "Do you feel confident in your ability to use the system for retrieving, sharing and storing information?" "Was the training practical?" "Were you left with any questions, and if so, what were they? The remainder of the questions focuses on the IT system. "Is the system efficient?" "Is the system accessible?" "Is it user-friendly?" "Is it useful?" The survey is complete and ready to distribute within an hour. Without wasting any time, Scott sends off the survey, company-wide. We all rush off to other meetings and put the Knowledge Management Project aside until the next day.

By the following afternoon, early results are in. I request a meeting with Nazari and Scott to analyze and discuss the findings. After computing a number of frequencies and descriptives, we're all in agreement; the survey yields no new insights. Staff is actually quite satisfied with their training. On the whole the company feels that the training was clear, practical and sufficient. Nazari is also right, though. A small minority of staff *do* have further questions and may need some extra help. But this really is the minority. Less than 10% to be precise. So this isn't the primary constraint we're looking for. Moving on we look at responses about the system itself. And still, the findings are uninteresting. Staff claim that the system is user-friendly and intuitive, just as Scott had predicted.

"Well, if nothing else we've managed to *eliminate* two potential constraints," I say, trying to find the silver lining. The others mumble a "yeah," but I can tell from their facial expressions that they were hoping for something more. I'm disappointed too. But it's getting late; nearly 7pm. Nazari and Scott head on home. I follow soon after, but my mind is still preoccupied with the KMP. I'm a problem-solver by nature, and this is a new puzzle. Puzzles like these are a large part of why I decided to abandon a medical career for a career in project management. The variety of problems that need solving, and the process of arriving at the best solution, is so fulfilling when things are right.

Chapter 2: Overcoming Self-Doubt - Reflections of a Less Confident Me

Sitting in traffic on my drive home, I can't help thinking more about how I arrived at this place in my career. Twenty years ago, working in a pharmaceutical company as a chemist, I would *never* have imagined a job where something like knowledge management of a firm would be my responsibility.

I remember having similar thoughts about 20 months ago, too, when I found myself tackling one of the biggest challenges facing the company at the time. This was back when there was no Strategic Project Management Office (SPMO). The challenge was quite simply that we had too many projects. Sitting in on some of the conversations around this issue, I wondered to myself how it was that *I*, a chemist by qualification, was contributing to issues on resource allocation and the business value of our enterprise project portfolio. My approach to work and to life is growth through learning. And to learn, I need to be able to admit fault, and sometimes even failure.

Our failure as a company was that we had lost focus, and had no way of measuring which projects were most important, and adding value. The employees were enthusiastic, but there were more good ideas than we knew what to do with. At times, it felt like every employee and their pets were working on some projects. But the company didn't have enough resources to effectively execute on every project, and so there were many zombie projects. Even for high profile projects, quality was taking a hit. We began to recognize that the longer term effects could be damaging to our reputation as a brand and to the financial sustainability of our company.

It was around this time that Bob asked me to lead the SPMO, and after some hesitation and encouragement from Bob, I agreed. Our first priority was to introduce a portfolio management approach to managing our pipeline of ideas and a growing list of active projects. We agreed that we needed to evaluate new projects and re-evaluate each of our current projects; as well as to be fiercely realistic about those projects that contributed to our organizational vision, mission goals, and objectives, and those that did not. All projects could not be a top priority. We needed to start saying "no" to those projects that were not strategically valuable, or risk the health of the broader portfolio. In a relatively short period, we were able to raise the threshold on approving new projects and close or delay many of the non-urgent and unimportant projects.

One program, in particular, comes to mind. This was a series of Greenfield projects in digital marketing using big data analytics; part of a plan to expand and supplement the existing business offering into new arenas. Unfortunately, the program was cut, along with a few other projects, after coming up short on a multi-criteria weighted ranking analysis; the results were quite eye-opening. Teams had been assigned, and many people had invested huge amounts of time and energy (almost two years actually) into these Greenfields, only to have the program pulled. But the decision was strategic. It had become apparent that while early entry looked like a good strategy for the emerging big data market, and while the digital marketing Greenfields were in fact looking as though they'd make an attractive ROI, we just weren't ready. And nor was the market.

The 'first to market' approach was misaligned with our strategy of growth within established markets. Our strategic priority had a clear focus on investing and directing resources toward our core business offering in markets that we were familiar with. The thinking around this was largely based on the elevated risks associated with emerging markets. Our company was known for high quality, guaranteed. Not for mistakes. So rather than enter early and stumble along the way with our competitors, we made the strategic decision to wait and learn from others' mistakes instead. To enter when we knew exactly how to position and execute on big data services in digital marketing.

But unfortunately, the realization of this misalignment between strategy and execution came after two heavy years of investment. The teams had come a long way and put in some serious hard work and commitment. They were personally invested in the program. And they were, not surprisingly, very disappointed when it was suspended. Of course, resources were not entirely wasted. The teams working on the program had learned a lot, and the company would retain this intellectual property. But ultimately this strategic shift meant a clearer measurement of project execution relative to its contribution to strategy. If the big data project had been assessed in terms of its strategic contribution sooner, then valuable time and resources wouldn't have been wasted. And we would have spared the teams who worked on the program, feelings of frustration and low morale. The suspension of this project had definitely made the teams involved, question the stability and solidity of our strategic direction.

Looking at the effect on our teams, I recall questioning why this misalignment wasn't identified sooner. I wanted to understand the underlying source of the problem. After chatting with people like Bob and a few other executives, my conclusion was that our portfolio strategy was not clearly defined, or well understood. A series of focus groups revealed that from top to bottom, at every level, staff had different perceptions of what the company's strategic vision actually was. And this meant that our people were working in different directions, rather than toward a common goal.

The executive committee and Senior Management then launched a number of workshops to refine the company's strategy, and to decide on a communication approach to ensure internal strategic alignment. Part of this involved cascading strategic goals, starting at the organization level, down to the functional heads, through to departments, teams, and finally to individual employee tasks and goals. Quarterly objectives, goals, and priorities were then set with this strategy in mind; and performance reviews became a regular opportunity to reassess individual and team activities and goals relative to the company's broader strategy. We also realized the need for a single body with a single leader accountable to oversee this strategic alignment at a portfolio level. This would increase the assurance that we can avoid repeating the same mistakes, such as allocating resources to the wrong kinds of projects. With some work, the days of Zombie Projects would soon be over. We needed a way of bridging the gap between strategic planning and strategic execution. And so launched the Strategic Project Management Office. The office that I head up today. I remember feeling so good about being part of the team that drove the positive change we now see in the company.

Baaaaap. The sound of a car horn interrupts my chain of thought. Darn. The traffic light is green and probably has been for a while. I feel a little embarrassed because I know how annoyed I usually get when other drivers do the same. I apologize to the guy behind me with a show of my hand and get going just before the light turns yellow again. Wow. All this reflection has made me quite exhausted. How did my thoughts even get me to this point? I was thinking back to over a year and a half ago, more or less the same time that the SPMO was launched. Time sure does fly. That was when Bob approached me for the position to head up the new office.

At that time I was so full of self-doubt about my suitability for the role. Portfolio Management was (and is still) new for me. I didn't feel ready, or sufficiently qualified. Sure, I had managed a $100 million portfolio for some time already. Eight years actually. The master data management and enterprise application development projects were some obvious successes for my career, too. And the new operating unit that I helped develop is now the largest and most successful unit in the company. But still, I knew of at least two other experienced candidates who were considered for the SPMO position, and they both held top program and portfolio management credentials. Other than an MBA, all of my certificates had the letters "Sc" printed on them - science. So I couldn't help wondering, why did the board choose me? I remember Bob explaining that it was because of my ability to effectively resolve conflict and lead teams. But I still wasn't convinced. I also worried that others in the company doubted my ability. I had even overheard a few of my colleagues questioning my appointment for the role. Despite my best efforts to ignore the gossip, this bothered me.

It wasn't until a conversation with Rebecca that I realized I was right for the role. She had so much experience in project and portfolio management, and I looked up to her as something of an expert. But one afternoon over coffee she told me the story of how she came to be a PMO executive and the local PMI chapter president. To my surprise, project management wasn't always a planned path for Rebecca either. In fact, her studies started in economics and politics. That's right. Inflation rates and presidential elections were her future. But as her career unfolded in the unexpected ways that careers do, she started to realize her passion and skill for planning and coordinating the bigger pictures. A move into a lead project role then evolved into program management, until she eventually found herself as the head of a major portfolio.

I'll admit I was a little disappointed at first learning this truth. Or maybe it was the feeling that I hadn't *truly* known her until just that moment. But as she continued her story I began to see how applicable it was to my own. "Don't let self-doubt, or the doubt of others, hold you back, Isabella," she said. "You are where you are because you're good at what you do. Some people study for years, completing one certification after the next, to become well-qualified portfolio managers, and still never make the cut. You're what we call an 'accidental portfolio manager'". And at that moment I knew she was right. I hadn't chosen this career path. The career path had chosen me. Lightbulb on.

The topic of certification did interest me though. At that stage, I had been considering the new Project Management Institute (PMI®i) certification in Portfolio Management Professional (PfMP®) for some time already. I first heard about the certification at a PMI conference that I had attended in the previous September. I hadn't acted on this interest because I was worried that the studies would be too much to take on over and above the pressures of my job. Of course, there was Rick and the kids to consider too. Fortunately, Rebecca had heard of a boot camp offered both in a traditional classroom format and also in a live-virtual forum where an instructor led a facilitated workshops online in real-time. I especially enjoyed the question and answer sessions; it was so valuable to have experts providing their insights. I chose the live virtual boot camp due to the distance and convenience. The best part was that it was all after working hours, which suited my schedule perfectly.

Taking that boot camp was one of the better decisions as it greatly accelerated the learning. Rick was very understanding too and really carried the family load for a few weeks while I got my head back in the study game. The workshops were manageable, but I had to put in additional hours to study the Standard for Portfolio Management, and focus on practice exam questions and the practical application of the tools and techniques. I told myself that if I was going to get that qualification, boy I was going to get it on the first try. The sacrifice paid off. I passed the exam on my first attempt, and I've never looked back.

The boot camp was excellent, and the confidence that I gained from the certification was invaluable. The training made me realize that I was already more of a portfolio manager than I knew. The theories and terminologies were sometimes a little new for me, but not their application. I had actually been applying the concepts in the Standard for years. Sure, there were areas where I needed improvement, and the certification gave me an increased awareness of these. Through the PfMP certification, I came to realize that I was always ready for the job, but now I had the credentials to back it.

Home at last. The garage door closes behind me and the day ends along with my reflections. I decide to call it a day.

Chapter 3: Addressing Big Challenges – How to Make Decisions Stick

The alarm wakes me, but I don't feel tired. The reflections from the drive home last night have left me feeling energized and confident. We will solve the KMP problem, just as we solved the issue with strategic alignment and too many projects two years ago.

I make myself a strong cup of coffee as soon as I arrive at the office. My meeting with Bob is getting closer by the day. Time to get serious about the KMP. The project is definitely aligned with our strategy, I have no doubt there. So what's the problem? What *is* the constraint to company-wide adoption that we're missing? I brought Nazari and Scott on board because of their closeness to the project details. So maybe it's time to try a different approach. Maybe we're *all* too close to the details. An objective view might be what we're looking for. So I start thinking of who else I can turn to.

I've learned the hard way that being inclusive when confronted with challenges works out a lot better than taking it all on myself. There's always Rebecca. Her experience as President of the local PMI chapter may have exposed her to problems of a similar nature. Besides, she's a lot more certified and experienced than I am. I don't know. Her expertise is quite specific to the construction industry. I decide that James is a better option. Managing a very large PMO in the global financial industry makes him a good choice for 'phone a friend.' I dial him up. The phone rings long enough for me to realize he's not going to pick up. Strike two. Who else? Then it dawns on me. Professor Woo. I decide to phone up my college professor, Professor De-Yu Woo. My formal studies ended what feels like a lifetime ago, but I still lean on his fresh perspective and wisdom from time to time. And this feels like one of those times. Finally, a stroke of luck. Professor Woo answers. I apologize for calling so early in the morning. He assures me that time is not an issue, but he's driving, heading on a camping holiday with the family, and so may experience poor signal at times. I can hear the kids giggling in the background. But I can't be picky. I'm happy to take whatever I can get.

The Professor listens quietly as I run through an overview of the KMP. How we managed to increase the budget and schedule to more accurately suit the project requirements, how successful the training has been, and most importantly, failure to get company staff to actually use the system. Finally, I share the not so enlightening results of the company-wide survey. Professor Woo waits until I'm finished. All the while his silence makes me feel uneasy; like I've missed something stupidly obvious. "I would like to respond with a question," he says, finally. I brace myself for something profound. "Why was the Strategic Project Management Office created?" That definitely wasn't the question I was expecting. I'm quite thrown, actually. What's the relevance of his question to my challenge with the KMP? The Professor must sense my confusion. He continues, "Was the company performing poorly before?"

I decide to adopt an open mind and satisfy what seems to be a massive sidetracking. I explain to Professor Woo that the company was actually very successful at the time of setting up the SPMO and had been for a relatively long while. New business was streaming in, turnover was healthy, and the internal systems were stabilizing. "Well then, he replies, "why did you and your company feel that this function would add any more value to an already successful consultancy?" I pause a moment to think. I guess I'd never really given it much thought before. What *was* the reason for establishing the SPMO?

I think back to nearly two years ago, to a time when there was no SPMO. Sure, there were considerations for the strategic alignment of internal portfolios. The SPMO was established to ensure that portfolios, and the programs and projects that they encompassed, would remain in tune with the company strategy. But aside from this issue, I told Professor Woo that the company wasn't doing too badly at all back then. In fact, profits were high, and business was booming. "Well then," he responds, "if the strategic alignment was the only issue, and you managed to solve it before the launch of the SPMO, why do you have a job now?" I smile to myself on the other end of the phone. I've actually missed the Professor's brazen way about him. "Tell me," he says. "What was one of the biggest obstacles you faced, or problems that you overcame, when first assuming your role in this new office? I can't believe that you've only ever experienced one challenge." He's right. And this is an easy question to answer. My next challenge was governance.

I talk Professor Woo through my thoughts as I recall the details around this challenge. Poor governance was one of the first problems that I discovered in my new role. Decisions about projects (their scope, their budget, their timelines, their strategic value, their measurement) lacked transparency. Executives and Senior Management often had pet projects that were driven more by personal interest than by company needs. What's more, is that there were nearly no objective and consistent way of evaluating these projects and their components in terms of their strategic value. And then there were those projects that *were* strategically beneficial, but incorrectly budgeted for, scoped, or running over deadline because Senior Management had extended the timeline. Without a plan to guide effective decision-making, executives and senior managers were taking a long time to make critical decisions or backtracked on previous decisions that had already been agreed upon. Decisions just didn't stick, and there was no consistency. And every time the project manager heard the executive words "I know it's not what we initially spoke about, but...", these changes caused heavy delays to timelines, and some projects even developed into Zombies - dead, empty projects that lasted forever but achieved just about nothing.

"You see, many of our projects were drawing in energy and resources, without contributing to the objectives set forth in our Project Management Plan," I explained. "We needed more structure and better management, oversight, and governance of the projects within our portfolios. Otherwise, we would continue to waste precious time and resources on projects that didn't give back". The Professor listened quietly. I only know he's still there by the occasional sound of a passing car and kid's voices in the background. "So I knew that the SPMO needed to take a hard hand and kill some of these Zombie projects off. Not all of them of course. We employed an objective measurement using multi-criteria ranking, and some projects clearly had to go. But there were one or two that we managed to bring back on track".

"One second please," he interrupts. I hear him whisper something about directions, probably to his wife. "Okay, go on," he says. "Tell me more about how you saved these projects that you identified as, well, worth saving."

"Okay, as I was saying, we managed to bring a few selective projects back on track. We started by identifying the project deliverables that were most important to the Sponsor, and the organization's mission. Once we had the priorities agreed upon and clearly defined, we set up a cross-functional project team to ensure a structured workflow and that there would be no further delays. Each team member was a functional expert, but also able to stand-in for other members as and when necessary. Daily fifteen minute stand-up meetings with this team provided the opportunity to work through any problems or issues and to review the status of risks. The result was a timely update to leadership on the previous week's progress. Feedback and insights were then offered by the Sponsor to keep the team aligned and on track with shifting priorities of the organization. We also established weekly measurable deliverables, each with their own clear, realistic and achievable end dates. These end dates were agile and adjustable, but only within the broader project end date which was "non-negotiable." Furthermore, these deliverables were integrated within the broader portfolio and deemed essential for the organization to achieve its strategic mission.

"Right.", says Professor Woo. "Now, when I asked you what your first challenge for the SPMO was, you quickly gave me one word. You said "governance." So how did the establishment of the SPMO help with governance?" I explain again that the biggest reason that we were funding projects with no strategic intent was poor governance and the lack of strategic oversight of our projects and portfolios. And that the SPMO would be a single body (led by myself), and working with a Governance Committee, to oversee key portfolio investment decisions going forward from that point. "The responsibility of the office is to see the bigger picture, while also recognizing the detail within it. To ensure that the projects that we invest in contributing to the broader company goals."

"Well then," said Professor Woo, "If that is your role, and the role of the SPMO, you simply need to do your job when it comes to the KMP." Professor Woo has always been very direct, to the point where some find him to be rude. But I've always appreciated this directness, and the time it saves to cut out the clutter. I take no offense at his response. "When it comes to the KMP, you are looking at the finer details, thinking like a project manager.", he continues. "You concern yourself with training, with the system interface, with budgets and schedules. This is good, but not good enough. Take a few steps back to see the bigger picture, the bird's eye view of both the tangible and intangible components that make this portfolio tick in tune with the strategy of the company. What are you missing that you won't find in the details? Have you considered-the--....".

"Professor Woo, you're breaking up," I try to say, just as the line drops. He must have driven through a tunnel or something. I guess I'll just need to use what I have from the call. But what does it mean? It's all quite vague really. Yes, I understand the project details very well. But what am I missing at a higher level? Strategic alignment? No, how could that be? The KMP is undoubtedly a move in the direction of the company's strategic objectives. I actually feel more confused than I did *before* the phone call. But, duty calls. I rush off to my first meeting of the day.

Chapter 4: Reframing Problems to Find Better Solutions

It's late when I get home, but the kids are still up and arguing over Lilliana's missing hairbrush. Kristopher is being accused of playing some sort of shady role in the matter. I instruct them to get themselves to bed, immediately. For once, they listen the first time around. I follow them to the bedroom, confirm that teeth are brushed, hands are washed, and tuck them in with a goodnight kiss. They probably have no idea that this moment has been the highlight of my day.

As I walk into the kitchen, Rick is taking out the dinner that he's kept warm in the oven. Lasagna, just what I needed! We sit down at the table with a glass of wine. "How was your day, dear?" he asks me. I suppose he can see that I'm a little tired tonight. I share my dilemma at work. Everything from the meeting the day before with Scott and Nazari, to the phone call with Professor Woo on my way to work this morning. "I just don't get it, Rick. And I *really* wish that Professor Woo had finished his sentence before the line dropped". Rick's face assumes something of a puzzled look as he nods his head. I can see he's still working through all the details of the narrative I just gave him. Honestly, he looks a little confused about it all. His experience lies in assisting startups, so the concept of a corporate level Knowledge Management Project is probably somewhat unfamiliar to him.

"Go on then," I say. "Let me hear whatever thoughts are ticking away in that head of yours." He smiles. "Alright. It might be a silly question though." I smile. "What is a knowledge management system *for*?" I don't think his question is silly. I explain that in a large organization, knowledge is in and of itself an asset. I explain the potential benefits to an organization when employees collaborate, the time savings when we learn from past mistakes, and the risk to the company if intellectual property disappears with a few essential team members who decide to leave. "Okay, I guess that makes sense then," says Rick. "I can see why you would implement this project, and I can understand the importance of getting it right. So how does it actually work then?". "Well, the Knowledge Management IT system is a large part of it," I explain. "This system helps employees and the broader company to identify knowledge sources, record information, share information, collaborate using shared knowledge and other very useful things. The system has been designed to be user-friendly and intuitive. The staff have all received training and have indicated that they understand how to use it for the purposes we've outlined".

Rick would like to know how we know for sure that staff understands how to use the system. "Because we've asked them," I'm proud to reply. I continue to explain how Scott, Nazari and I developed and distributed the survey, and then analyzed the results. Rick rubs his head. I wait for him to share his thoughts again. "I'm obviously pretty removed from it all, so I'm just putting this out there dear," he says, "but did you happen to ask the staff if they understood *why* they had to use the new Knowledge Management IT system? I mean, you explained the business benefits of knowledge management pretty well to me. But do *they* understand these benefits? *I* didn't know until now.

I think for a while. He's got a fair point. The staff definitely understand how to use the system, but they might not understand *why* to use it. It dawns on me that we didn't include that question in the survey. But why not? Well, because Scott, as the IT guy, brought the IT questions to the table. And Nazari, as the project manager, brought the practical, training questions to the table. But what perspective did I bring? Maybe that's what Professor Woo meant. *I* need to be the one to think at a higher level, a portfolio level. That's *my* job. Scott, Nazari and I had all *assumed* that the staff understood how the use of the system would benefit the company, and their ability to perform in their jobs. Knowledge Management is a term that has been thrown around the office a lot over the past year. But that doesn't mean that the people who are actually tasked with implementing the system understand why they should be using it. And I know that *I* wouldn't take the time to use something if I didn't understand the purpose behind it. So why would the rest of the company? They're all intelligent people, and we need to treat them as such.

This system wasn't intended to be a one-off event. No. This needed to be integrated, ingrained into the staff's daily workflow. Formal and informal processes for sourcing, recording and sharing information needed to form a part of our organizational culture. The obstacle is not the training or even the system at all. No, there is a cultural obstacle. I need to work to transform the organizational culture, to make a clear link between the use of the IT system and the connection with strategic objectives. This way, employees will be informed, and more likely to buy into the knowledge management IT system. They'll be more inclined to take the time to use it effectively.

I'm just starting to get lost in my thoughts about shifting the culture, creating an understanding of the positive implications of using the system, and earning staff buy-in, when my phone rings. I glance over and see the name "James Fischer" flashing on my screen. I plant a quick kiss on Rick's cheek and whisper "thank you darling" just before picking up the phone. As I suspect, James is returning my call from earlier today. The timing couldn't be better. "James!", I say, "How are you?" He's been consumed with work; the acquisition of a competing financial institution has had a few complications that have kept him pretty busy lately. "Enough about me," he says. "I need a distraction. Please tell me that you have problems too! I'll feel so much better" he says jokingly. This is so typical of James. Always more excited to solve everyone else's problems before his own. I very willingly tell him about my challenge in getting company staff to use the Knowledge Management IT system.

After catching him up on the survey results, I explain my most recent realization. "We've identified the main obstacle to be organizational culture. The staff is not incorporating the system into their daily routines because they're not understanding the importance of why they're using it in the first place." And this is where I could use his advice. "James, any suggestions on how I could shift the thinking and the culture would be much appreciated."

James is not short on ideas. "Have you tried focus groups to understand the staff views and misperceptions about the application?" I explain that we've monitored use of the system and sent out a company-wide survey, although I already recognize the limitations of both of these as I'm talking. The feedback is shallow. In order to get deeper, more informative feedback, he recommends that we start with a series of focus groups. "Listen to them, understand what their existing thoughts are on the system, what misperceptions they might have about the usefulness and rewards of using the system." I grab my tablet and start scribbling down some notes. I like the direction this is taking. "Then, once you have a clearer idea, use the results to target and address the specific misconceptions by holding workshops. In these workshops, have a knowledgeable facilitator guide teams through exercises, like brainstorming the potential benefits of the knowledge management system for their team performance, their individual performance, and finally, for the company as a whole in terms of achieving its strategic objectives. It's important that they come to the answers themselves. That's how you'll create your buy-in". James' advice makes sense, and it comes from years of experience in leading large numbers of people through organizational change. I'm looking forward to turning this advice into action.

Chapter 5: Beating the Competition to Market

I wake up the next morning feeling fresh. I'm ready with a plan based on James' suggestions from yesterday evening. As soon as I get to the office, I call in Callie Smith, my administrative assistant. I ask her to set up a meeting with Scott, Nazari, and Human Resources for the afternoon. All the right heads to arrange the Knowledge Management focus groups and workshops. I'm feeling a lot better about my meeting with Bob next Monday. We may even have some positive results by then.

I've just leaned back in my chair with a sigh of satisfaction when Richard Quan pops his head through the door. Richard is the Portfolio Manager for New Product Development, one of the portfolios within the broader enterprise portfolio. And Richard is one of the many capable colleagues who makes my job a whole lot easier. One of his most significant projects at the moment is a new management tool for Vendor Governance and Risk Management (VGRM). It's unusual to find him at my office outside of scheduled meeting times. He's not usually one for 'sudden drama.' So I know there must be a real problem.

"Hi Isabella, sorry to bother," he says. "Is now a good time?" I can't help but giggle a little to myself. As if there's ever a "good time" these days. "Of course, Rich. What can I help you with?" I succumb with a smile. I join him as he takes a seat at the small table in my office. "Well, you know that new management tool that my team's been working on for the past while? The VGRM tool?" he asks. "Yes, it's about five months in the pipeline now, isn't it?" I say. "Yes, exactly," he says, excited that I'm so up to date. "Well, as you say, we've been working on this thing for close to six months already, and now we've got trouble. We've just found out that our main competitor will be coming out with a similar tool in the next four months".

This tool was supposed to be a significant move for our company. It would be one of the most effective and comprehensive products available in the market, and a number of our key clients were collaborators in this endeavor. This is a single management tool that would combine the need for vendor governance and the associated risk management in the supply chain capability. Some of the key benefits would be automated requirements mapping, compliance and security reporting, analyses for measuring vendor criticality, and a number of other uses. A progressive management product that would be a valuable competitive advantage for our clients. "The problem is," says Richard, "according to our capacity and projected timelines, we'll only have this tool ready to hit the market in eight months' time." He rests his chin on his hand. "I could really use your thinking around this."

I'm intrigued by this dilemma. And I've got some immediate ideas. "Right," I say, thinking out loud. "So the first option that springs to mind is to continue our existing timeline and hope that our competitor fails to deliver. But that could result in wasted resources should our competitor actually pull through. And we risk clients turning to the competitor before we even make it to market. Still worse, we could lose valuable clients who start to take all of their business over to the 'other side.' So that's not an option". "Exactly," says Richard. "The other route," he adds, "would be to cut the project altogether and admit defeat. The problem with *that* course of action is that all five months' worth of resources invested in this project would be down the drain. Plus, our clients who collaborated by contributing to the requirements will surely be upset. And if we're realistic, we would probably need to launch a similar tool in the future *anyway* - if not for competitive advantage, then for competitive parity".

It becomes clear that the only way to maximize the return on the investment that we've already made into the VGRM tool would be to beat the competitor to market. "Well then, Rich, this leaves us with one choice it seems. We need to shift the timeline so that we're able to launch the management tool before our competitor does. I'm thinking an adjusted deadline of just three months". "You know, I was afraid you'd say something like that," he says jokingly. "I think I knew it was the answer, but I just needed to hear someone else confirm it. It's a reduction in the timeline that's not going to be easy to sell to the team". We both acknowledge that the team is probably not going to take kindly to skimming five months off of their project deadline. But we'll just need to make it work. The question *now* is how best to approach this.

Richard and I start by brainstorming some of the main obstacles and risks to meeting this shorter timeline. Richard explains that he's been struggling to keep track of the project progress. "We're measuring performance regularly, of course, both for team members and the project as a whole, but the measurements just aren't holding any meaning or value. And they don't seem to be motivating team performance either". So the first obstacle is establishing rudimentary performance metrics that are measurable and accessible. So we need to relook at when and how we measure performance. "Good. What else, Rich?". "Well, if I'm very honest about it, we're using second-class resources on the project," he responds. "You and I both know that the best talent in the company is dedicated to client assignments. Of course, I understand that this is strategic. Clients need to get only the highest quality service. But it would be great to have one or two top Solution Consultants working on this VGRM tool. With the shorter timeline and our existing team, I fear that the rush might compromise quality. Having some of the best on the team might help guarantee a quality product, despite the tight timeline." "I agree with you completely," I say. "But I think there's more to that. Clients get the best talent, a strategic move for sure. But I think you'll also find that the best talent *wants* to work with clients. Client assignments are generally more interesting, more challenging, and hold better financial rewards and recognition than our internal projects do. So even if we got clearance to move some of our best Solution Consultants onto this project, it may be a challenge convincing the consultants themselves to get involved". Richard agrees. He's scribbling furiously on a small notepad that he's pulled from his pocket.

"You know, I think you've just touched on something else, Isabella," says Richard, without looking up from his notepad. "These two obstacles may even be related. If we can start by revolutionizing the performance metrics, and we could do this in such a way as to make them attractive to our best talent, then we may just be able to convince the Solution Consultants to *want* to work on this project". I like his thinking. I see the sense in it. A re-design of the reward and promotion system that accounts for internal contributions as equal to, if not more important than, client contributions. "Okay, then we need to start by changing the performance metrics, next, get sign-off for using the top talent on this project (as an exceptional case, of course), and then convince the consultants themselves to join the internal project team. We've got a rough plan of action. We'll need to get some other expertise around the table, though, before we can get much further. HR, Senior Management, the Project Sponsor, and Client Engagement Partners come first to mind."

By the next day, we have everyone in one room. I foresee some conflicting interests, so it's going to be an interesting meeting. Straight off the bat, Client Engagement is against the idea. No surprise there, really. They're not interested in losing any of their key talents, and their reason is that "Top talent is for top clients. Without clients, we have no business. As it is you've got our teams running around attending focus groups and workshops over this whole knowledge management thing. We don't have the capacity to spare". Richard and I are already sensing that we'll need to escalate to the Director of Client Engagement, Rina Shah. She's usually very reasonable. Fortunately, we have Human Resources present too, and they have a few good points that swing the thinking. "This would be a good growth opportunity for the consultants, and a valuable opportunity to diffuse external knowledge within our internal project teams. A little bit of mix and match from time to time could go a long way toward creating more innovative thinking for both teams." I add that this wouldn't become the norm. This project is high stakes for us, and we can't afford *not* to deliver within the next three months. We could even lose a few important clients if things went wrong, which might mean the loss of the very external projects that our Solution Consultants so enjoy working on. Finally, we have everyone on board. Senior Management is in favor, and Human Resources is committed to assisting with new and improved performance metrics. The Governance Committee is happy with the approach and offers to provide any other support necessary for the three-month completion.

I have to rush off for a check-in with Scott, Nazari, and Human Resources, who apparently have good news about the KMP and the workshops that they've been facilitating. It turns out that James' advice was golden, and employees are coming up with some really valuable insights about the benefits of using the system. With any luck, we'll see increased adoption within the next one to two months. My meeting with Bob isn't looking too grim anymore.

Chapter 6: Winning Over Top Talent

The next afternoon sparks the first day of the next three months as we work furiously toward the completion of the VGRM tool. This project will take priority for a while, of course. Richard has already debriefed his team on the project changes, including the dreaded three-month timeline. He felt strongly about breaking the news to them before they heard any rumors via the grapevine. The worst communication is sometimes no communication. By positioning the revision of performance metrics and the addition of new team members as a solution to the tight timeline, he managed to get them all on board. Initially, I had my concerns that bringing in Solution Consultants would offend or demotivate his existing team. But fortunately, they were quite enthusiastic about their new team members. With the adjusted three month deadline, they're probably just grateful for any help they can get. Now we've got one week to get the new, expanded project team together, including the addition of two of our Solution Consultants currently assigned to client engagement projects.

After chatting further with Richard and Rina, we agree that Matt King would be an ideal candidate. While Rina would certainly feel her loss in Client Engagement, Matt is the most talented consultant on her team, and she realizes he may be the necessary talent we're looking for on this project. I used to work with Matt back when I was on client engagement projects. Then already, he was dedicated, driven, and fantastically smart. We'll approach him directly with the proposal. To secure the second addition to Richard's team, the project role will be pitched to the remaining Client Engagement teams as an opportunity to work on something different - a challenging, internal project.

We know that we'll need to work on shifting the negative mindset that skewed the perception of internal versus client engagement projects before we can expect to get full buy-in. But we also know that we need to move quickly. So Rina, Richard and I decide that there's no better time than right now. A coffee meeting is booked with Matt to try to get a feel for his interest in the project. We figure that if *he* is interested, the many consultants who look up to him might be interested too. We head down to my favorite New York cafe, and after some friendly catch-up on work and life, Rina introduces the idea to Matt. And what a *mistake* we've made. "Rina, you *know* how much I enjoy working with our clients. It's my passion, and heck, it's what I'm good at. Am I missing something here?". "Not at all," responds Rina pleadingly. "You're in the top performance rankings in our team, so this is not a reflection of your value or your work. It's not a punishment. In fact, it's quite the opposite". I decide to weigh-in in an effort to clarify the situation. "Matt, Rina has had nothing but excellent feedback about your ability. And that's actually the entire reason why we've approached you. This project may be internal, but it's also going to be extremely challenging, facing a tight timeline, and requiring the highest quality. Ultimately the VGRM tool will be made with clients, for clients. So we need the best on this project". "Yes, but it's *not* client engagement," says Matt. "So why pull me off an important project that I'm already invested in with my current team?" Rina, Richard and I try a few more angles, but ultimately the meeting ends with the single highlight being the delicious lattes. I quickly realize that there *is* a better time than right now. And that we shouldn't have approached Matt until we had the new performance metrics and reward system figured out. We decide to hold off on further chats with Matt or any other Solution Consultants until we have a thoughtful and attractive proposal.

The following morning Human Resources, Rina, Richard and I are on the performance management framework. Richard starts by explaining some of the current shortcomings he's been experiencing with the performance metrics. "Internal or external aside," he says, "the metrics have not been valuable in tracking progress. And now, more than ever, we need less rudimentary, more informative and more meaningful metrics that will make sure we're on track for launch in three months". I completely agree with him. We've got to be accurate. Together we come up with a few ideas for improvement, and Richard makes plans to work with HR to get the metrics refined over the next two days. Linked to this is the other very important issue at hand, which is redesigning the reward and promotion system for internal projects. We need to change perceptions such that this internal project is weighed equally, if not more heavily, compared to client engagement projects. The question is, what is the best way to do this? We start by breaking down the reward and recognition structure currently used for talent working on client contributions. Solution Consultants are naturally attracted to working with clients, and we want that same level of motivation on this internal project. Incentive pays, networking, and a history of greater career growth are the key drawcards for client projects. *These* are the attractions that we need to work into the VGRM tool project.

Incentive pay is something that we can definitely incorporate into the pay structure for the project. For every milestone that is achieved, and that passes the quality check, all team members will receive a competitive financial reward, or perhaps a sponsored trip away once the project is completed. Return on investment measures for the project can be linked to post-completion rewards for the team. This project will not directly lead to networking opportunities, but we agree that we could promote the recognition of the best team members on the project through special credit on the tool information page. Furthermore, we could reward excellent work by giving top team contributors preference for lead positions on future client projects. "Well, things are already looking far more attractive for Matt than they were yesterday," I say. Rina and Richard agree. We're all feeling more confident about pitching the idea to Matt and others from the Client Engagement teams. Richard says he'll get this all drawn up and documented before the close of business today so that we can start conversations again tomorrow.

Tomorrow comes around in no time at all, and it's Friday. A perfect time to get Matt and other Solution Consultants interested in the project, and the attractive new reward structure it offers. Well, perhaps I'm biased about the reward structure. But Richard's told me that his current team members are more than happy with it. Anyway, Matt will have the weekend to think it over, and with any luck, we'll have our project team by Monday.

Ping. I see a new message from Rina. She says that she and Richard have done their best to pitch the idea to the client contribution teams. They're on their way up to my office to report back. I find myself quite literally crossing my fingers. I hear Callie greeting them both as they walk in. "Well?" I say. "Give me the good news. How did it go?". "So much better than expected!" says Richard, with a look of relief. I smile broadly and wait eagerly to hear the details. Rina explains that many of the Solution Consultants had some great questions, which seemed to indicate that they understood the challenge and value of working on the project. "They were definitely not averse to the reward structure, either," adds Richard with a smirk. "It looks like we did a good job there." In a way, I'm not surprised at the positive outcome. What makes our top talent so incredible is that they are driven by good challenges. These teams are competitive and *want* to achieve the impossible. So while the tightened timeline might make our current project team a little shaky, it's actually appealing to the Client Engagement teams. "Only one problem," says Rina. "Matt," I preempt her next words. "Exactly," she says, "He's still not convinced. But he says he'll take the weekend to think it over". We agree that we'll need to make a call by Monday, with or without Matt. Time is of the essence. And besides, if he really doesn't want to be involved in this project, then forcing him is not the solution. As always, we need team members who are invested and *want* to be on the team. "Hopefully we'll have more than one applicant from the rest of the Client Engagement teams by Monday," says Rina. "They really did seem interested in the opportunity."

Happy with the progress we've made, and choosing not to let Matt stress me out, I clock off early. I'm fetching the kids from school today, and then we're off to dinner and a movie. Strangely enough, I might just be more excited than they are. I wish the others a good weekend as we leave the office.

Chapter 7: Embracing Change on a Very Good Monday

The weekend has been a wonderful distraction from the busy week before. It's Sunday, and while the men struggle desperately to watch the football game *and* the barbeque at the same time, the ladies are discussing work. There seems to be a unanimous feeling that Sundays are 'blue' days. The days when they all feel a little down because they know that they have work tomorrow. I understand what they're talking about, I do. I've had those days too in the past. But right now, I can't help but disagree. Because to be honest, when it comes to Sunday blues, I rarely seem to have them anymore. The others laugh in disbelief. But I mean it. Sure, my job isn't without its stresses, but it's stimulating, fulfilling, and it's what I love. Okay, so maybe I sound like a cliché. But even as I think of the pressures of a three-month deadline for Rich's team, and working with Rina to transform top talent attitudes toward working on internal projects, I'm excited. I'm *really* excited. I guess I'm one of the lucky ones. Rick says it's not luck. "You've followed your passion, been brave, and made some serious career moves, dear. You worked hard and took chances to get where you are today", he tells me as we clean up the aftermath of four families, including six children and two dogs. The truth is, he's been a big part of that. My career has definitely taken a toll on our marriage at times, and Rick wasn't always happy with the amount of time I chose to invest into my job (and take away from my family). I don't blame him really. But we've found an understanding now, and I think we're happy. And so the 'not so blue' Sunday comes to a calm end.

After a relaxing weekend filled with family movies and barbeques, Monday blasts me into the new week. We have five, yes *five*, applications from the Solution Consultants. Rina and Richard obviously did a killer job with the pitch on Friday.

Together with Human Resources, they'll screen the applications and choose one (or two, depending on Matt) of the best. I've had an email from Matt saying that he'd like to chat with Richard and me this morning. I'm hoping he's made a decision, whatever it may be. It's time to move on.

Matt is the first to arrive at my office for the meeting. We share stories from the weekend until Richard walks in. I can tell that Matt is eager to get started, so I decide to get to the point. "So Matt, thanks for initiating a chat this morning. I'm guessing you've had some time over the weekend to consider our proposal? What are your thoughts on joining the team on the VGRM tool project?" He smiles nervously before answering. It's not a common thing to see Matt King feeling uncomfortable. I'm intrigued. "I'd love to be a part of it," he says, quite shortly. Rich and I are not far from stunned at his complete turnaround since last Thursday. "That's excellent," I say after a few seconds of disbelief. "Can I ask what changed your mind?" "Well, that's sort of why I wanted to give you my answer in person," he says. "I want to apologize for being so narrow-minded when you first approached me. And I don't want you to think that I'm only on board with the rewards structure. I'm not opposed to it, obviously. But the rewards are not my primary motivation for accepting." Richard tries to tell him that we don't require a justification for his decision, and are just happy to have him joining the team. But Matt marches on nevertheless, "You see, the truth is that I overheard some of my team members talking at lunch on Friday, you know, after you pitched the project to them. I expected to find them talking about how upset they were about the whole proposal. But instead, they were talking about *me*. Someone mentioned that they thought I found the idea of working on internal projects to be "below me." Another agreed and said that it's probably because I prioritize my own reputation and recognition. That I'm not much of a "team player," and don't see the benefits this would have for the internal teams, and the company."

By now Richard and I are all ears. This is a whole new level of sensitivity for Matt, and certainly not what we were expecting. "I realized that the only performance metric that I usually fall short on is my peer rating for teamwork. I achieve my project targets without fail, and client feedback is consistently positive. But my peers don't always seem to share the feeling. So, to keep growing and improving myself, I need to actively work in this development area. And the VGRM tool project is the perfect opportunity. I can use this opportunity to share my client knowledge and experience with your project team, Richard. And at the same time I can assist the company with their timely achievement of an important product and work on my teamwork skills. It's a win-win. It might even show my Client Engagement team that I trust them to deliver top results on the current client project, and that they don't need me to do that."

"Well, we're only too happy to have you on the team," Richard replies. Richard and I are just thrilled that he's changed his mind and that he's motivated to be part of the project. We are yet another step closer to achieving that three-month target. I thank them both for a great meeting and express my excitement at the outcome. But now I'm off to a lunch meeting with Bob for our usual check-in. He mentioned that he has something in particular to chat with me about. It sounds ominous, but I'm not going to waste energy worrying until I know the details.

After pushing through the lunch hour traffic, I arrive at the restaurant at the same time as Bob. We sit down, and Bob orders his usual, the rotisserie chicken salad with extra dressing and a Diet Pepsi. After placing my order, we jump in with the first agenda item. This, of course, is the KMP. Bob was part of the Governance Committee who approved the increased budget, and he's concerned that we're not seeing the expected return. The last report clearly indicated that employees were not integrating the system into their daily functions. I'm pleased to give the update that things are looking up for the KMP. "With the help of Scott Rogers and Adena Nazari, the IT system was successfully completed, employees well-trained in its use and functionality, and more recently we've started to see an increase in system use and reporting. Its early days since the focus groups and workshops, but the evidence is pointing toward an improvement, Bob. I'm confident that the next report will show a more positive picture". He's happy to hear this, and finds our approach with the workshops and creating employee buy-in an interesting one. I also update him on the VGRM tool. "We've now got two of the best Solution Consultants on the team, Matt King and Tamara Gonzalez. Three months is looking more achievable." He nods his head a few times as I talk. "It sounds like you're on the right track, but you're still dealing with a very tight deadline," he says. "It might be worth critically reviewing the major risks of this project. Having a client contributor pull out, or Matt falling ill, you know, some of the nastiest situations, may just be a make or break for this project hitting the go-live deadline". Bob's got a great point, and something I'm sorry to say I hadn't thought of myself. I make a note to follow up with Richard on this.

"Now, I've got some exciting news for you," he says keenly. This must be the mysterious agenda item, the specific "something" he's been wanting to talk to be about. I can tell from his facial expression that the news isn't going to be anything bad. "The company has grown tremendously," he says "and I think it's time we start thinking about improved integration between our core business processes. At our next executive committee meeting, I'd like for us to make the business case for an Enterprise Resource Planning system (ERP). I'm talking about a deep, strategic integration that connects many of the core functions and processes." I think this is a great idea, and I agree that we're at the right place in our maturity to be thinking along these lines. But this is going to be one hell of a program. "That's for sure," says Bob. "So we'll need to put together a convincing business case. Let's start with the ERP Vendor. I'd like you to do some research on this, and present your proposed vendor at the Executive Committee (ExCo) meeting this week. Perhaps start by reviewing some of the vendors our clients have used in the past?" I'm familiar with ERP planning and implementation, of course. I've assisted clients with ERP implementation in the past. But this has always been with the help of consultants and other experienced stakeholders. Responsibility for the successful implementation of our own ERP is going to be a first-time experience for me. And I'm both nervous and excited at the same time.

Chapter 8: Pitching Enterprise Resource Planning (ERP) System to the Executive Committee (ExCo)

It's been almost a month since Bob first mentioned the ERP, and my review of potential ERP Vendors has gone well. We've worked with a few excellent vendors on client projects before, and based on this, I've managed to narrow down my list to just two vendors who I'm confident would be a smart choice. Actually, considering criteria such as vendor age, past clients, pricing and tier, my first choice is clear. This is a Tier II vendor with cloud-based ERP experience and expertise. Their software is only moderately complex and is specifically designed for mid-market companies like our own. Also, their initial and annual subscription fees are less expensive than most of the Tier I ERP Vendors. I've managed to get Dane Chang's thumbs up on the choice as well. He's been fundamental in his role as Chief Technology Officer, and I value his understanding of the technical requirements. I'm feeling good about the ExCo meeting this afternoon. Besides the Vendor, I've worked with a few key people within and without the company to put together a rather thorough business case for a strategically integrated ERP. I'm feeling confident.

Bob leads the ExCo meeting as usual, and after a few other important issues are concluded, he raises the business case for an ERP system across the company. He begins by positioning the need for such a system, and the benefits it could offer us. "We've grown tremendously, and we continue to grow. But as we grow, we're seeing increasingly that processes are being duplicated, reporting is absorbing too much capacity and in some cases not sufficiently flexible or suitable, and we have large amounts of data at risk of becoming out-of-date, or worse, lost altogether. Implementing an ERP system is what we need to improve our efficiency, secure and accurate data, streamline processes, and ultimately reduce time and costs through improved decision making. Additionally, this system will allow for effective collaboration and communication with our clients, partners, suppliers, and internal departments". A few attendees are immediately on board. Some even say that they have recognized the need for an ERP system over the past six to twelve months, and are fully in support. But, an ExCo meeting never goes quite as smoothly as planned. With a number of intelligent perspectives around the table, there are bound to be some constructive debates. Of course, these usually lead to the best possible outcomes.

A select few are concerned about the large costs, business disruptions, and organizational change often involved in an ERP system primarily at the implementation phase. Beyond the costs of the implementation, they are worried about the amount of time that will be taken away from key staff who are pulled into the implementation team. "This could cause significant delays to our client projects, Bob," says someone. "That's true," he replies. "But while we will be placing additional pressure on a few areas within the organization during the planning and implementation of the ERP, the benefits will be reaped by the whole organization once complete. This is an investment. Isabella and Dane have also done some solid research into possible vendors. I believe that if we secure the right vendor and software, we can minimize these direct and indirect costs and reduce the timeframe for deployment". It looks like it's my turn to weigh in. "Exactly Bob. We've managed to find what we believe is a good option. If you would all please take a look at the ERP Business Case Report that you'll find attached to the agenda, and go specifically to the section on Vendors. You will see that our first choice is an experienced cloud-based ERP Vendor, with a great track record. They are Tier II, and so less expensive than Tier I solutions. But their software is a fully configurable cloud-based solution, which means quicker to deploy, more accessible, faster, and more seamless integration than traditional systems. Their interface is also very intuitive to navigate, which should reduce our training costs during deployment". Someone raises concerns about compliance and security of information. But I remind them that cloud-based systems have less than 40% of the initial implementation costs of traditional on-premise ERP systems, are more flexible, and can be managed more easily by the service provider. I add that once we have invested in a traditional ERP on our premises, moving over to cloud-based in the future is going to become a costly transition *anyway*. So we should start the way we intend to finish. A few more executives are convinced that a cloud-based ERP system is the way to go, and in the end, majority wins. But Bob makes it very clear that, despite the feeling by some that this is still the wrong decision, the ERP implementation is bound to fail if executives are not seen to be in support of it. And then we are sure to waste company funds on a failed investment. "So as leaders, we *all* need to present ourselves as supportive of this project."

The next debate is about the ERP subsystems (e.g., micro-verticals), and the order in which we should implement them. It becomes clear that while most are in favor of an ERP, there is a division on the purpose behind it. Some are arguing that Bob's plan for a strategic ERP integrated throughout core processes and systems is unnecessary. Their view is that a more tactical implementation would do the job to replace some of the more outdated systems and increase IT support. Fortunately, a large majority disagree - including me. "The system alone will achieve little if we don't actively pair it with business process improvement and a transformative approach. And for this kind of strategic implementation we require all subsystems relevant to our core business to be prioritized," I plead.

After some further banter, I convince everyone to use a multicriteria weighted ranking analysis, so that we can quantitatively make an informed decision. Drumroll please... we make the call to take a strategic, rather than a tactical, approach to the ERP. The subsystems that we identify include Human Capital Management (HRM and Payroll), Financial Management (General Accounting, Accounts Payable, and Asset Management), Client Engagement Management, Corporate Performance and Governance, and Reporting (as both standalone and integrated throughout other systems). I raise Project Portfolio Management as a potential sixth subsystem, but the rest of the committee seem to view this as "straying from our core process." I disagree, of course. But I decide to leave that battle for another day, despite my strong views on the matter. In terms of order of implementation, a few feel strongly that Reporting should be the last subsystem to be implemented, given its necessary integration with other subsystems. Some others believe that Reporting should in fact be more focused on Business Intelligence and Knowledge Management Systems, and should thus be implemented with urgency; that this subsystem will inform the implementation of all other subsystems. A little more back and forth, a quick pair-wise analysis, and we arrive at the decision that to be good stewards of our resources, we must redesign our chart of accounts and company structure. Doing so means this will be the big "T" (Transformation), to include process redesigns and organizational transformation. All agree Financial Management and Reporting will be the first micro verticals to be implemented. More discussion ensues, and the team decides that an iteration of the two will include Corporate Performance and Governance, and Client Engagement Management. All seem to cautiously support Human Capital Management and Payroll as the third iteration; all except for the Vice President of Human Resources who is pleading for iteration one, so they can sunset their mainframe HR System. From our consulting practice, we all know the challenges that accompany enterprise

HR projects. It was further agreed that the ERP implementation should adopt a program management method.

Finally, everyone is in agreement and has committed to fully supporting the planning and implementation of the ERP and all its subsystems. I am tasked with leading the initial ERP planning and implementation internally, including securing our ERP Vendor, an experienced ERP Implementation Partner to oversee the project, and a strong Program Manager to lead this program. While executive buy-in and sponsorship is the first battle won, I know I have my work cut out for me for the better part of the next year. Even though the plan is to hire a Program Manager to lead the day-to-day management, I'll need to be intimately involved in the planning and allocation of resources at the portfolio level. My broad responsibilities are now to ensure strategic alignment and resource sharing through my role on the Executive Committee and to oversee risk management, resource management, big issue escalation, implementation methodology, performance management, and organizational change management. But before I can do any of this, I need to ensure that we have our chosen Vendor, an ERP Implementation Partner, and a highly competent Program Manager. They should be able to provide more guidance regarding projected timelines, resources, methodology, and implementation accelerators so that we can begin planning and building our team.

Our choice of vendor is available and eager to assist. They will provide the cloud-based software, assist in provisioning and deployment, and manage the system upgrades remotely. That's one move in the right direction. Next, I need to identify the best possible ERP Implementation Partner. The firm will need to bring experience, skills, and focused accountability for the successful planning and implementation of the ERP system. This should reduce the risk of anything going sideways. I know of one or two "million-dollar" lawsuits against vendors where ERP systems took years to implement and then failed anyway. That is *not* going to be us. I decide that a referral is probably the best place to start. I know that James' company has been using an ERP system for some years already. He may be the right person to ask. I pop him a quick email and also asked for his thoughts on a program manager.

James responds within about half an hour and with a strong referral. Dinika Naidoo is the ERP Implementation Partner that he worked with on the initial implementation of their ERP system some years back and again when they did the move over to a cloud-based system earlier this year. She was referred to him by one of his clients, and he has been very satisfied with her services. James describes Dinika as being highly capable, honest, and very experienced in ERP project and program management, both traditional on-premise and SaaS cloud-based. I'm sold. I thank James, give Dinika a call, and mention that I'm a friend of James'. She's definitely interested in the collaboration, so we arrange a coffee meeting for Thursday. Unfortunately, James doesn't have a good recommendation for a program manager; his favorite consultant was just assigned to work on another program at his company. I thank him, again, for solving another one of my challenges. A handy friend, indeed. He laughs, tells me that he's always happy to help where he can.

Now, what to do about the program manager. This ERP program is going to be big, it's going to be complex, and it's going to need someone with experience and credentials. Experience and credentials, I think to myself. Oh! What about Rebecca? I know that she was closely involved in managing the ERP at the construction company she works with. And from what I remember, the ERP had a strong strategic focus. She's been incredibly busy lately, though. Well, I suppose there's no time like right now to find out. I call her up and see what her schedule is looking like. "That sounds very exciting, Isabella," she says, "but unfortunately I'm committed at 100% capacity for the next twelve months, at least!" I sigh, hopelessly. "That's fine, Rebecca. I had a feeling you were going to say that. Any chance you can recommend someone else?" She gives me two names and contacts. I spend the rest of the afternoon continuing the search but to no avail. Finding the right fit for this program manager role has proven to be exceptionally difficult so far. Anyway, at least I have a good lead for the Implementation Partner.

Chapter 9: Setting the Stage for ERP

Shoot! My meeting with Dinika is in less than an hour, and I'm not even out of the driveway yet. And where on earth is my phone? I saw Kristopher playing with it last night... Ah! I hear it ringing! Naturally, I find it buried between the sofa cushions. Its Terrance Lee calling, a college senior that I've been mentoring since he joined the local PMI chapter. I'll give him a call back later when I've got more time. Right now I need to rush.

I'm lucky. The traffic is better than usual, and I arrive only two minutes late. Dinika is already sitting at a table outside. I recognize her from her profile picture on LinkedIn. "Hi, Dinika? It's so great to meet you", I say introducing myself. We shake hands, and I apologize for making her wait. "No, that's okay," she says. "I only just arrived myself." And *that* was the start of a very satisfactory meeting. The conversation evolves quite naturally. I'm pleased to find that Dinika has relevant industry experience, impressive ERP knowledge, and even boasts one or two connections at the chosen vendor (likely to be beneficial at some point in the implementation). She also says all the right things to make me believe that she'll be a good fit with the team culture. I appreciate the transparency in our conversation. "Our firm's not cheap, but we're very good," she tells me. "I appreciate that the implementation of an ERP system is large, it's complex, and it interrupts the workflow of every employee and process. So, my approach is collaborative. The more aligned and integrated the team and the company, the stronger the chances of a successful implementation. Well, that's my view." I like her view. I can't help but agree with her view. We chat a bit more about the role that her firm would play. "We would act as a primary liaison between your company and the ERP Vendor to ensure that timelines remain on track, and possibly even expedite where we can. We'll also take the lead in program and project management oversight for the internal ERP and vendor teams and organizational change management". I explained that this program is the "BIG T" (transformation). Dinika smiles and offers "Our firm has solution consultants with deep industry knowledge who can help with business process redesigns, lead the system configuration, and shepherd the initiative through the Conference Room Pilot to System Integrated Test and Go-Live." With a short pause, she says "Further to this, we also offer a Post Go-Live service where we can administer and maintain your system, and this at a fraction of what it would cost you to hire and train an IT staff to cover the footprint we've been discussing." I leave the meeting feeling positive about the new relationship. But, to make sure it's not just the high from caffeine we'll screen a few more potential firms.

I've also chatted with Richard about the program manager role, and he suggested that we promote internally. He recommended Cecilia Rothschild, who recently completed a prestigious certificated called the Program Management Professional (PgMP). Given the potential for Dinika's firm to take on some of the program management responsibilities especially with the vendor, I think we'll create a solid program leadership team managing both internal and external activities. Clear division of responsibilities will be vital.

The next big move is to introduce the concept of an ERP implementation to the company. I know that it's critical for everyone to understand what's coming, and more importantly, that they see how strongly the leadership supports the decision for an ERP system. We decide to hold a mandatory company-wide information session, and together with Bob, explain the risks and benefits of ERP. Bob kicks it off by making it very clear that this program will be costly, will require change and flexibility, and will (to different extents) involve every person in the company. But, if the company pulls together, the outcome will be future cost savings, more streamlined operations, greater flexibility in service offerings, enhanced benefits with more integrated features, and informed decisions that ultimately improve our competitiveness and benefit everyone in the company. I also introduce the idea of bringing an Implementation Partner on board and the role that they'll play in the process. "We'll be working with a firm recognized as leading experts with ERP implementation to make this as smooth and seamless a process as possible. There will of course still be some significant changes to our own internal teams and responsibilities, as people are called on to assist with the ERP program. And in these cases, it's incredibly important that we support each other".

After the session, Bob and I open the floor to questions. I already sense some resistance from Scott Rogers, based on the questions he's asking. He seems anxious about the foreseeable pressure on his team when it comes to the IT side of the implementation. And yet at the same time, he seems to be upset that he was not included in the selection of the ERP Vendor. He is concerned about company adoption, given his recent experience on the KMP, and feels that choosing the right vendor will play a big role in this. I assure him that we will do everything in our power to manage the workload for his and other teams; and that we will be meeting with all key team leads soon, including IT, to discuss details about the ERP program. I also promise to chat with him separately after the session, so that we can talk through the features and benefits of the chosen ERP vendor. Most of the other questions are inquisitive, constructive and informative. Communicating fast and frequently will be our first step in effectively managing the ensuing change. I dare not use this forum to raise the managed services that I discussed with Dinika, as it stands, several IT resources on Scott's team have earned the nickname "server huggers", as they just don't seem to understand the value and benefits of cloud computing, and fear this as an easy way to outsource their jobs.

Things have started to move quickly since then. It's only been a week since I first met with Dinika, and she's already met with the Project Manager and Steering Committee. Furthermore, her firm has been approved as the choice for our Implementation Partner to assist with the ERP. I'm thrilled. But now we have the difficult task of putting the right internal team together, a strategically selected team of people dedicated to, and responsible for, successfully planning and implementing the ERP system. After much back and forth, and a very messy looking whiteboard, the team structure is decided upon. The internal Implementation Team will include a Program Manager (Cecilia Rothschild), and project coordinators, functional managers from each subsystem (HR, Finance, Client Engagement, Governance), IT experts (Scott Rogers), and team leads from Business Analysis, Business Engineering, Development, Quality Assurance, Deployment, Operations, and Training. Dinika recommends a cross-functional team, because ERP is not solely an IT responsibility. It requires intimate involvement from functional managers above and beyond the inclusion of technical team members. I agree completely, having worked on projects in the past where problems like scope creep arise because the functional perspective was excluded from the Implementation Team. Each team lead will take ownership of their process. The Implementation Team will report into the ERP PMO (including myself and Dinika), who in turn will report to the Governance Committee (Bob as Sponsor, and the Steering Committee consisting of myself, the Chief Financial Officer, Dane Chang, Rina Shah, and the Chief of Talent). The vendor team will include two consultants from the ERP Vendor Company. And Dinika will be working with me to guide and assist in the process and spearhead the ERP program.

In an initial meeting with the Implementation Team, Governance Committee, Vendor Consultants, and Dinika, we agree on the project scope, timeline, and budget. The ERP program will consist of three sub-programs: 1) business process improvement, 2) organizational change, and 3) information technology. The program is estimated to run over a period of 18 months, excluding one month for planning. I emphasize the point that the ERP system is a strategic move, not a tactical restructure, and so we *must* plan to do a thorough job of it. "We are aiming for a strategically ingrained and fundamentally practical system integration, not a superficial change. So, we'll need to give this 18-month program our all. It *will* be tiring, and it *will* be tough, but we need to resist the temptation to take shortcuts". Everyone appears to be in agreement on this point, but I'm still getting the impression that something's a little off with Scott. Much of the meeting is also spent considering how involvement on the ERP program will affect the team's fulfillment of their primary roles and responsibilities and the contingencies that will be put in place to account for this time. Rather than full-time, dedicated program roles, we agree on an 'open access' approach. At times this will mean reassigning primary responsibilities to other team members not directly involved in the ERP program. At other times we may need to outsource help. But in all cases, we'll need to think ahead and think strategically, about the planning and implementation phases of the ERP. Dinika and Cecilia will create the first draft of the Requirements Traceability Matrix, Risk Register and Project Charter of Requirements to guide the Implementation Team in their work. A clear Communication Plan is also established. This includes a 20-minute standup meeting with the Implementation Team three times a week and a weekly war room session with the vendor consultants and Dinika as a space for constructive debate and collaboration. The Steering Committee will meet with the ERP PMO, and reports and updates on the scope, budget, and deadlines will be distributed to all relevant parties, including the Sponsor, every month. Dinika has committed to consolidating bi-weekly reports from all functional teams to present to the Governance Committee.

By the end of the week, I'm officially exhausted! It feels like I've done more planning and strategizing, and attended more meetings than I usually do over a period of *months*. I'm relieved that it's the weekend. But I feel like I've forgotten something. Terrance! Ah, I feel terrible. It's after 6pm on a Friday evening, but I figure I'll give him a call anyway. Terrance answers after the first ring, "Hi Isabella." "Terrance, I'm so sorry to only be returning your call now! There's no excuse for it. How are things going on your side? How were your exams?" He laughs lightly. "No problem, Isabella," he says sweetly. "My exams went very well actually. I even managed to nail that Finance course I told you about. I was *so* relieved". I congratulate him and ask him how his project is going. As part of his final year, Terrance signed up for an experiential learning course for which he needs to participate in a real project running over 11 months and covering a number of strategic and project management principles. He has the role of Project Manager. And this is usually where he seeks my advice. "Well," he pauses with a sigh, "that's actually what I was calling you about." "We're just over halfway with the project now, and we've done some really great work up to this point. The food bank is really happy with the planning we've done for the next fundraising event. But the project is not over yet, and I can feel my teammates slowing down. Exams were exhausting, and the energy just isn't there anymore". I listen to his familiar story with sympathy. "Last week we even had a bit of an argument between two of our teammates. Joe forgot to get quotes from the caterers, and Mary just flipped. The poor guy did apologize, but he also made the mistake of blaming his forgetfulness on being tired. Mary promptly told Joe that his excuse was intolerable because we're all tired. But Mary also had her share of difficulties too. Mary was working with Patricia Johnson, another volunteer at the foodbank responsible for the marketing creatives, and Mary gave the wrong dates causing some delays. So when Joe reminded Mary of her missteps, both were fired up. Anyway, Mary and Joe are refusing to talk to each other, which you can imagine is making collaboration almost impossible. I don't know what to do".

I tell him that I can relate completely and that exhaustion and conflict are completely normal when a team gives a project their every attention over a prolonged period of time. "What your team needs is strong, focused leadership, Terrance. And I believe you are able to offer that leadership". "Thanks, Isabella. I appreciate that. But honestly, I have no clue where to even start", he says. "Well," I say, "the first step would be to remind your team that they are a team and not a group. They are a bunch of connected people working toward a shared goal. And they are more likely to achieve that goal as a collaborative team, than as a group of individuals. The next step would be to remind them why they are on this team in the first place. What is the purpose or gain that you are all looking for? Is it as simple as a passing grade for graduation? Or is the team aiming for an "A" grade on this project? Maybe it's even less about the grade, and more about the valuable learning gained by giving this project your best shot? A way to prepare for the real world? Anyway, the point is, you need to all understand your purpose and goal, so that you are aligned with your efforts and motivations". "Thanks Isabella. I'm taking notes", says Terrance with a hint of excitement in his voice. I smile to myself.

Mentoring Terrance is always so rewarding. "Any advice on what I should do about the clash between Joe and Mary?" he asks. "I'm really stuck on that one!" I scratch my head as I take a moment to think. "Well, if I were you," I say, "I would avoid singling Joe and Mary out, and instead get the whole team together. Then, do a fun, personality activity. I'll send you the link. This activity is quick and easy, and helps team members to understand each other's personalities, preferences, and approaches to work. By being aware of these differences, it enables individuals in the team to approach others in the most constructive way for their particular personality. I've tried it out with a few of my own teams before, and it's a winner". "That sounds great Isabella!" he says. "Okay Terrance, I've got to run, unfortunately. I'm fetching Lilly from ballet. But please let me know how everything works out. I'd really like to know". He thanks me again and agrees to give me an update next week sometime.

Chapter 10: Returning to Work - More Puzzles and Problems

It's been three weeks since I've been at the office. Mom's been really ill, so we flew down to be with the family. She seems to be recovering nicely now, but the doctors have warned us that it'll take some time for her health to fully return. She's old, I know. But it's never easy when the realization sets in that your parents won't be around forever. Dad's taken it all quite badly too, and now I'm not too sure how he'll cope if anything more serious happens to Mom. Nearly 60 years of marriage... after a lifetime partnership like that I can't really blame the guy. Anyway, Mom and Dad are going to come and stay with us for a while until she's back on her feet again. It's going to be, well... "interesting" in a word. But my sister is in no position to take care of them, especially with all the traveling she's doing these days. Of course, the kids think it's just fabulous that Nonna and Gramps will be "sleeping over." It's amazing how kids always find the brighter side of everything. Well, everything except bedtime.

So I'm feeling a little emotionally drained today, but I'm relieved to be back at work again. Something to take my mind off of things back home. I also know that I've got some serious catching up to do though; this week is going to be challenging. The ERP Implementation Project has already kicked off (I Skyped in for the first meeting). Since then there've been regular team meetings, reports, and updates. I've tried to stay on top of it all as much as possible, but it wasn't easy to do remotely; especially at my parent's place which is about as technically smart as the dark ages. But the team's made some good progress. They've identified the main risks to the ERP implementation to be lack of user adoption, over-customization, resource availability, and the leaking of sensitive data. For the first risk, we've learned our lesson from the KMP.

We'll be sure to adopt a robust organizational change management approach, to address the all too common dip in productivity when systems go-live. This means choosing a modern, user-friendly interface, providing sufficient training, *and* ensuring that every person understands the importance and benefits of actually using the ERP system. We'll also be sure to keep the system simple and focused on core processes that support the critical success factors for the program. And all sensitive data will be flagged ahead of time and assigned a 'guardian' to oversee the implementation tasks that touch on those data points. As for resource constraints, well we've struggled with various options for the lead team members. For the Subject Matter Experts, we've settled on the notion of "Full-Time Access," meaning the SME's get to keep their day jobs, but be available to the project team when needed.

Another major progression of the program has been Dinika's initiation of business process transformation ("the BIG T"), and her request for the functional teams to conduct an analysis of their business processes. We discussed that many of the teams are not trained in process inventorying, mapping, or analysis, so we've arranged for Dinika to lead a number of training sessions. My focus from an SPMO standpoint is on a strategic, transformational ERP, rather than a superficial technology update (aka. "Lift and Shift"). So I'm fully in support of a thorough business process transformation to accompany the new system. I've also asked all of the teams to attend master data training to ensure that we establish accurate and relevant data standards. Depending on the ERP system, we may even launch a project to define and implement master data. Lastly, the Implementation Team and Vendor Consultants have attended a team building workshop to set mutual expectations, form connections, and motivate and align everyone in the same direction.

But, as positive as this all sounds, not everything has gone smoothly. As I suspected, Scott has started to demonstrate more obvious resistance to the ERP program, and this has largely been manifested in his attitude towards Dinika and her team. "He's been an obstacle in almost every training session, Isabella," says Dinika, sounding frustrated. She's the first person I scheduled to meet with today. I wanted a full update on the training. "He usually doesn't participate, and if he does, it's more often than not to argue against the training content, the activities, or to criticize our decision to move to the cloud." She takes another sip of her coffee before continuing. "And I'm all for constructive debate. I really am. I appreciate it as a tool for learning and innovation. But unfortunately, Scott seems to be influencing his team as well. We've heard some negative comments about the ERP coming from his team in the IT department." Unfortunately, I can't say that I'm surprised at this news. But I'm a little disappointed in myself for not following my gut and clarifying things with Scott sooner. Of course, my absence over the past few weeks hasn't exactly helped, either. I tell Dinika that I'll sort it out immediately, and apologize for the hassle. "It's no hassle, Isabella, I'm very used to this sort of thing. But, I will say that I'm glad to have you back!" Dinika says with a smile as she leaves my office.

My logic tells me to chat with Dane first. As Chief Technology Officer, it's largely his responsibility to demonstrate his support for the ERP vendor and to be sensitive to his people's attitudes toward the same. From my engagements with Dane, I'm certain that he's on board with the program. Actually, he's one of the ExCo members who seemed to advocate for the ERP from its very first mention. So whatever's causing Scott's negativity is likely stemming from some other person or experience. I manage to squeeze in a quick chat with Dane in the afternoon, and he confirms Dinika's challenges. It seems that Dane's been fielding some concerns from his department too. A number of his people have been worried that the ERP will result in their roles becoming obsolete. And this anxiety is probably the source of the resistance that Dinika is dealing with in the training workshops. Naturally, they are resisting what they view to be a threat to their careers. "Of course no one's wanted to get him into any trouble, they're a tight team, but Scott has clearly been at the root of their concerns," says Dane. "He's off today, but I'll chat with him first thing tomorrow." I thank him and ask him to let me know if he needs any support.

In the meantime, I've got another issue on my hands. A black swan that we never saw coming on the Vendor Governance and Risk Management (VGRM) tool project. In an email I received from Richard yesterday, he mentioned that one of our biggest client contributors is requesting an exclusive Intellectual Property (IP) and non-compete agreement on all definable contributions of content. With the help of people like Matt, we've managed to remain on schedule with the project and are successfully closing in on that three-month go-live deadline. We've looked at the options, and at this stage, it's too late to replace the client's contribution and create our own unique content. We'd almost certainly miss our deadline. We'd also be risking a healthy relationship with a long-standing client if we don't come to some sort of compromise, and fast. So, we'll need to start and conclude negotiations with the client as timeously as possible. Richard, Bob and I have a meeting with them in the next few minutes. I take one last quick bite of my energy bar and head to the meeting room.

The situation becomes clear very quickly. It seems that our main contact at the client company failed to get the right sign-off before embarking on the collaboration. And this is where the sudden request for an IP and non-compete agreement is stemming from. After some polite negotiation and a reasonable attempt by Bob, they told us that they were not interested in continuing the collaboration. The words come as something of a shock. All that time and all those resources, just to pull the plug. I can see that Bob is growing increasingly frustrated with their stubborn stance on the matter. Rather than risk an argument, we thank them for their time and bring the meeting to a close. "We're not speaking to the right people Isabella," says Bob as soon as they've left the room. "None of those guys were present for the initial negotiations on this project. We need to get in a room with Ajen Pather. He was key in confirming this collaborative agreement, and I *know* he's got sway at the company. And you know what, if it comes to it, we'll hold them to a minimum payout for the investment already made in this project. I don't want to go that route, but I will if I have to." Bob's angry at the situation, and understandably so.

The next day arrives, and Dane comes through on his promise to chat with Scott. Their conversation has shed some light on Scott's anxiety, and Dane believes it would help to get the three of us in a room together to set some of his misperceptions straight, including the direct implications of the ERP program on Scott's team. I think it best to start by finding out where Scott's misplaced attitude toward the ERP has come from. "Scott," I say, "before I jump into the impact of the ERP program on your team, I'd like to hear what your own thoughts are on the system. What is concerning you and why?". "Well they're not good," says Scott quite directly. He never did have much of a filter. "And I have evidence to back it. I spoke to my friend Steve Jackson - he's had tons of experience with the implementation of ERP's - and he says that they always take the biggest toll on the technical teams. They undo all the work that's already been invested in the current systems, even though the current systems work just fine. And most of the time all of that effort in updating the software actually just results in some sort of meaningless facelift, anyway -- and do you really trust the cloud?" Ahuh! It's all starting to make sense to me now. "Thank you for sharing your honest views, Scott. Your friend, Steve's, experiences are unfortunately quite common. And I can see why they would make you skeptical of the ERP system implementation. But I do wish that you had come to chat with Dane or me sooner. You see, many companies do tend to focus on a technical "makeover," as such. But we're not looking to apply lipstick here. Our goal is deep, and it's real. We're aiming to make a noticeable difference in the company, one that will improve the work processes and data management of every job and department, including *yours*. What we're doing is a strategic imperative, one that will impact the firm for the next 10 to 20 years." Dane nods in affirmation. "This is a massive undertaking, and we need smart, committed people to lead this change and ensure its success," adds Dane. "So Steve was right in that regard. We undoubtedly need your team's help. And it probably *will* take a toll on your team's workload. I'm not going to lie to you. But please know that Isabella and I will do everything possible to create as smooth and manageable a transition as possible. And when this is done, you will be one of the champions who successfully led this change. The very change that will keep our company a leader in its industry". I agree, and make it quite clear that both Dane and I believe in the vision for the ERP.

I also address the issue of the team and the anxiety that Scott has been spreading. "Just to be clear, there is no danger of roles becoming redundant or obsolete here," I say. "The system will change, but we will still very much need the skill and talent that our IT department offers. This value will just be leveraged within a new system and structure." After running through some of the specifics of Scott's responsibilities and input areas on the ERP, he seems to be convinced of his long-term relevance, and that his team will receive the support they need as they take on additional responsibilities on the ERP. But he's still a little hung up on the cloud option. I sense that this will take further discussion. But for now I can see that he's reached his maximum point of absorption, so we'll pick these conversations up again at a later stage.

Another day is done. Crazy. Sometimes I can hardly believe how quickly time flies. And then, of course, there are other times, when hours drag on like some kind of bad comedy show. Like when I get home and have to deal with noisy kids, needy parents, and a husband who's equally unhappy with the current home situation.

I walk through the door and immediately make my way to the bedroom to change my shoes. Those heels were killing me! I know they look great. But I just can't believe that humans were ever meant to walk on those things. I throw on a pair of flats and grab my keys. "Kristopher, let's go," I yell down the passage. "Coming mom," a little voice replies. Kris has recently started guitar lessons, and Rick's got a teleconference, so I'm on driver duty. Not that I mind much. I actually appreciate the alone time to just be still and reflect. When the weather's good I take a walk in the school gardens for the fresh air and leave my phone in the car. A whole hour to myself. What a treat!

Today is one of those good weather days. It's Spring, so the garden smells amazing. Too bad the pollen gives me a stuffy nose. I pull a tissue from my blazer pocket, and Dinika's business card falls out onto the damp ground. I must have forgotten it there after our first meeting. As I pick it up, my mind unwillingly drifts back to the office. The VGRM tool has been successfully launched, on time, and it's a massive hit. We managed the issue with our key contributing client. We came to a favorable agreement where the client will retain IP on a particular part of the risk model, and our firm will pay a royalty if we sell and use this with other clients. As for the rest, we've managed to negotiate a shared IP agreement, and their attorney dropped the demand for a "non-compete." What a relief that was! The tool has brought in a ton of new business, and our client contributors are happy. Matt was a huge asset to the project. His peer ratings were still far from perfect, but he was satisfied that it was an improvement from previous projects that he's worked on. He also had a positive effect on some of the others, and one internal project team member in particular performed fantastically. Richard has referred her to Rina to lead one of the upcoming Client Engagement projects. So, all in all, the project was a measurable success for our company, for our clients, and for the individual team members.

Scott has made a turnaround on the ERP, too. And quicker than I expected. He's known to be stubborn, even difficult, and he's definitely got to let his "cloud" fears go, the snide comments are frustrating. If he wasn't so darn good at what he did, he may not be in the position he's in. But unfortunately, his attitude has also created a ceiling to his leadership growth. Anyway, at least his energy is now constructively channeled toward the ERP, and not aimed at obstructing its implementation. Dinika has reported that the whole IT team has been more willing to learn since Dane chatted with them as well. I'm still not completely comfortable with the way things are going on the program though. We're now three months in, and the system seems to be taking shape as something quite complex. It's that typical situation where the foundation looks straight, but the wall comes up skewed. Now that we're well into implementation, the problems are becoming visible. I'm especially concerned that we've strayed from our initial, simple focus on core business processes. Each team lead has made small additions after small additions, leading to an unnecessarily intricate system. And yet, while we've possibly included too much, I'm also aware of the opposite.

Scope creep has arisen exactly where I thought it might. It's becoming increasingly clear that requirements management should have been more tightly integrated with project management. Projects, programs, and their successful execution are a huge part of what we do. Internal or external, projects are an integral part of what we do. Of course, I tried to raise this months ago when we were deciding on the scope of the ERP. But, requirements management and the use of a traceability matrix was thought to be too heavy-handed. After all, we're a world-class firm, some believe we're just inherently gifted. Now, the unwanted system complexity that has developed on the ERP program has become the very evidence of the necessity of requirements management and a formal process for proposing changes beyond what was initially included in the Program Charter and the Requirements Management Plan. The introduction of Governance would also provide for more structure along with integrated change control. When reviewing some of the proposed changes, it was quite concerning that Purchasing thought they should proceed with a process change without seeking the approval of Accounts Payable. This is what we do, and they're acting like it's the first time they've heard the term "Purchase to Pay." Okay, back to the fundamentals, for both the Project and Product, we've decided to build multi-level Work Breakdown Structures (WBS). The Business Analysts for each of the work streams will own the WBS, WBS Dictionary, and Work Plan for the ERP configuration and the Project Manager will incorporate those milestones into the overall work plan. This way the ExCo will have greater visibility into the overall status of the ERP Program. This is especially critical as we measure earned value and estimate to complete. Bob has started to come around to this thinking now, too.

But, altogether this scope creep means something complex and difficult to implement beyond the "Big T" we were anticipating. I know we'll need to pause the program and do a thorough clean-up of the ERP requirements. This will mean cutting out the requirements that either don't add value or aren't solidly anchored to the ERP Program Charter, as well as perfecting our internal integrated change control and Governance processes. Our Implementation Team has been working long, hard hours on their ERP responsibilities for the past six months. And we've really felt a strong investment from the rest of the company, too. Amazingly, everyone has really come together to support the successful implementation of the ERP in any way they can. And now... well, now I'm about to ask them to undo some of that hard work. And then, I'm going to ask them to do even *more* work by briefing them on the criticality of thinking like an integrated organization rather than the silos they've grown accustomed to. Let's just say that I'm not going to have many fans when we're done. I know that I need to guide, motivate, inspire this company for another year or more in order to see the ERP successfully implemented and engaged. So however I go about this, I'll need to take an approach that doesn't jeopardize the trust and respect that I currently hold. I'm just not sure what that approach actually looks like in practice.

"Mommm!" I hear behind me. It's Kristopher. The hour has somehow flown by me, and his lesson is already over. "Mom, I've been looking for you everywhere!" he says. "Sorry darling," I say apologetically. "How was your lesson?" As we walk to the car, Kris tells me all about his cool guitar teacher, and how he "totally dominated" the new song he's been learning. By the time we get home, Rick has already started dinner. I offer to help but get interrupted by my dad calling from the lounge. It seems he's forgotten how to use the remote again. Rick shakes his head. The plan for mom and dad to stay with us for a few weeks has turned into almost five months, and it's taking its toll. Mom has recovered nicely, and the doctor says she's fit to stay on her own again. But she and dad keep finding every reason not to leave. I think it's all the time they're getting to spend with the kids. I know I should be firm with them, and tell them that they simply have to go. After all, we've done so much for them already. But it's so hard to push them away, especially with the grim reality that they're old and not going to be around forever.

I help my dad with the remote and then go to the bedroom to charge my phone. The stupid battery seems to be dying every 8 hours lately. Anyway, I should be due for an upgrade soon. I'm just about to leave the bedroom when my phone beeps and pops up a reminder for Prof. Woo's birthday. I better just give him a call now before it's too late in the evening, or I forget. "Isabella, hello," he answers. I can immediately hear the hum of conversation in the background. He must have people over or something. "Hi Professor, I'm just calling to wish you a happy birthday," I say. "Oh, thanks," he says. I ask him about his day, and he explains that he used most of it to visit his favorite museum and library in Manhattan. "Anyway, I don't want to keep you," I say, mindful that he has company. "Oh please," he says, "I've been listening to my Aunt Anne complain about the food since four o'clock. Tell me how things turned out with that project we spoke about last time". I laugh at his disregard for Aunt Anne's palate and update him on the Knowledge Management Project. I tell him that my call with him, and a subsequent chat with Rick, helped me to figure out that people didn't understand *why* to use the system, even if they understood *how* to use it. I also explain how I realized that my role is to understand the detail of projects, but also to avoid becoming so engrossed in it that I can no longer see the bigger picture. He's pleased with the positive outcome and is happy that he could help. I know that it's probably a cheeky move to pull on his birthday, but I decide to touch on my most recent issue as well. I explain the scope 'clean-up' and refocusing required on the ERP program, and how anxious I am about not damaging the trust and motivation of the company when I announce these changes. Prof Woo listens attentively and then recommends that we fully explain the importance of an integrated system, not only in terms of company benefits like cost reductions and improved margins but also in terms of the benefits to the teams of employees actually using the system by streamlining work processes and delivering organizational efficiencies. He says that we should emphasize that it would be simpler and more useful to create a system that focuses specifically on core processes versus expanding the scope to include those on the periphery that add substantially to the cost but result in little overall value to the organization. Then, in accounting for differences in opinion about what actually constitutes "core," he suggests ranking processes for identifying system components and add-ons that are core, and those that are not, and the latter's need to be removed from the program scope. Before he can finish, I hear someone calling his name in the background. "Thank you so much for your advice, Professor," I say. "It's always a huge help. Now please, go and enjoy your birthday!"

When I get downstairs, everyone is already at the dining table eating. I join them and say how great the food smells. But I can see from the look on Rick's face that I'm in trouble. A relatively awkward dinner ensues. Eventually, the kids and my folks go up to bed and Rick and I are left alone. He gets up and starts walking over to the kitchen with the empty plates. "Rick, is something bothering you?" I ask after him. I'm always the first one to address an issue. His default behavior is the silent treatment. "Well, what do *you* think, Isabella?" he says as he starts to pack the dishwasher. I grab my plate and walk over to him to pack in the machine, but he takes it from my hand and tells me to "just leave it." "I'm not a mind reader Rick. If you're unhappy with something I've done, you'll need to tell me what it is," I say, starting to get frustrated. "No, Isabella. The problem is that you're so blind to what's happening here in the first place, that I actually need to spell it out. Your parents, as much as I love them, have overstayed their welcome. I'm working, I'm raising two kids, and now I'm caring for your elderly folks as well. I take them to the doctor, I cook, and I shop. All you do is escape to work, come home late, and then continue work on the phone while the rest of us eat dinner together as a family. I'm sorry Isabella, but *this* is not working for me." Wow. When Rick finishes, I'm short of words. I know that he's right, and I feel awful. But I also don't know how to fix it. It seems obvious. Send my parents home and work normal hours. But in practice, those things are really hard to do. I try to tell him that it's only for a short while longer, but he's tired of hearing that answer. Eventually, I say that I'll get my parents moved home this weekend but that I am going to stay with them for two nights to get them settled in. It may make the transition easier for them. That's all I can think to do right now. He replies that it's "fine," without turning to look at me.

The rest of the week has been fairly miserable. I've been trying to spend more time at home, but I'm getting the silent treatment from Rick. And then there's Bob, who's really been applying pressure on me to refocus the ERP program scope as soon as possible. The Governance Committee has been disappointed with the last two status reports, so I guess he's been getting a mouth full too. I've asked him to give me the weekend to consider the best approach. I know that one of my biggest faults is how affected I am by other people's disappointment in me. I hate letting people down. And now I feel like I'm disappointing everyone. My husband, my parents, my company. I need to get over myself, fix the issues that lie before me, and move forward. When I arrive home, mom and dad are already packed and waiting in the lounge with their bags. They seem a little down, but I know that my going to stay with them for the weekend has eased the blow. Lilliana is crying because she wants Grampa to stay. The general mood just feels really, well, low. "Lilly, please don't cry," I plead with her. "I promise that we'll visit Granny and Grampa all the time. It won't be long until you see them again, my girl". I know it's not something that I should admit, but I'm almost glad to be leaving for the weekend. Rick helps me pack the bags in the taxi, gives me a rather cold kiss on the cheek, and tells me to have a safe flight. I promise to let him know when I arrive.

It's dark by the time we pull into the driveway. Mom and dad quickly get settled into their own space again, and I unpack my things in my old bedroom. This time I've come prepared so that the WiFi issues don't get me worked up. I send Rick a message to say that we've arrived safely, and his little profile picture catches my eye. It's a photo of the two of us and the kids at our last family holiday with big smiles on our faces. We had so much fun that summer. I can't believe how much Lilliana has grown since then! I fall back onto the bed and take a deep breath. I know that I need to be there more for the kids and Rick. I don't want to look back one day and think, "My, how they've grown." I want to be an active part of their growth and change, and the people they become. It's only fair to Rick, too. I know that I'll need to set some boundaries at work and be okay with leaving the office before my to-do list is entirely ticked off. I'll also need to be more present when I'm at home and not let my mind continuously wander off to problems and complexities at the office. Anyway, I know that I'm my own worst enemy when it comes to setting boundaries.

I make a quick lasagna, but it tastes nowhere near as good as Rick's. In fact, it just makes me feel sad. Afterwards, mom and dad say goodnight and head off to bed. I'm tired, but I sit for a while longer by the TV. The reality show that my dad likes to watch is only half way through. It's mostly rubbish, but I find myself watching anyway. They're interviewing a man who was recently retrenched because his role was made redundant. The man felt unfairly treated because he fully believed that the role he played and the projects he worked on were beneficial to the company. He felt that he was not treated fairly because after everything he had given to the company, all the long hours he had worked, nobody gave him the opportunity to motivate for his own relevance. Of course, I don't take these kinds of shows too seriously. But it did get me thinking. Maybe the best way to decide which components of the ERP system to do away with is to ask the people who thought of them in the first place. To give the Sponsors and Team Leads the opportunity to motivate for the relevance of these system components to our core processes. This, together with a few critical criteria for review, could be the best way to help Team Leads to understand precisely *why* we have to undo some of their hard work. A long yawn makes me realize it's probably time for bed. I turn off the TV and call it a night.

The next morning I wake up late. I can hardly believe that it's nearly 11am already, except that I forgot to put the blinds down, so the sun is streaming into my bedroom. I can also hear my mom singing outside my window. She hasn't wasted any time in tending to her garden, which has been hugely neglected for the past few months. I pour myself a cup of coffee, kiss my dad good morning, and walk out to the garden. "Morning," my mom calls to me with a smile. "Can you believe the state of my roses?" Funnily enough, I think they've enjoyed coming home more than they thought they would. And mom's seeming healthier than ever. It's great weather in the open country. The sun is shining and birds singing. I could almost forget what an emotionally stressful environment I've come from. And yet, I feel eager to get home. I can see that my parents are going to be fine. Besides, my sister's promised to check up on them during the week. I need to get home to sort out my own family, mend things with Rick, and start a new, more balanced approach to work on Monday. I think I'll leave early tomorrow morning and surprise them. Maybe we can do something fun, like the food market.

The next morning I'm on the road before 7 am. On my way back I stop to get pastries from our favorite roadside stall. Maybe I'll make it home before they've had lunch. When I open the front door the kids are still running around in their pajamas, and Rick is sitting at the table in his gown reading the newspaper. Lilliana is the first to see me. "Mommmy!" she shouts with excitement, as she launches towards me. I give her and Kris a big hug, tell them that I missed them, and watch as their mouths water for the delicious treats I've bought. They run off to the kitchen to fetch plates. In the meantime I walk over to Rick, give him a kiss, and tell him that I've missed *him*, too. He keeps silent. "I'm sorry," I say, as I figuratively stuff some humble pie into my mouth. "You were right. My parents were here for way too long, and I'm not here enough. Retreating to work has been the easiest escape. But I promise I am going to try a lot harder, starting today." Rick finally looks up, gives me a smile, and says that he's sorry too. That he understands the kind of pressure I've been under at work, and he knows that I love my job, but that he loves *me* and wants to feel close to me.

That night, once my head hits the pillow with Rick's arms around me, I fall asleep so quickly that I can't even remember my last thought.

Chapter 13: Confronting Another ERP Challenge - Resources

I've had a surprisingly productive month, even though I've been spending less time at work. I really have been trying harder to make time for Rick and the kids, and we seem to be doing much better. Mom and dad are happily settled back into their home too. So my personal life has gone from being the source of all stress to relatively stress-free.

On the work front, Dinika, Cecilia and I have followed Professor Woo's advice. We've done a thorough assessment of the ERP system and its components, and identified the key criteria for a component relating to core processes. Using those criteria, we've identified those requirements which seem to deviate. Each Team Lead was then reminded of the original ERP program scope, its focus on core processes, and the benefits of keeping the system simple. For any deviations from our 'core process criteria,' we asked the Team Leads to submit a written justification for the component's relevance, which had to be approved by integrated change control. A few surprised us and agreed up front that they realize they've strayed from what was most important. Some submitted strong justifications for continued work on these system components, and others, not so strong reasonings. But, at the end of the day we were able to agree on those system components that needed to be delayed or killed, and those that should continue, without destroying the respect or motivation of our teams. Because people understood the reasoning and felt that they were fairly treated for being allowed the opportunity to make their case, the team morale has improved vastly. Now, about three weeks down the line, we have streamlined energy toward the initially-envisioned simple, focused, and user-friendly ERP system.

This scope 'clean-up' has come at a cost though. While we were working to identify those system requirements that were core and to manage attitudes around this, we were forced to pause some of the projects within the ERP program. And this meant that we lost precious time. We also added a layer of Governance requiring a review by the team lead, which has now been incorporated into the program structure. Overall, we'll be slapping on an unforeseen three months to the program end date. But this is not our only problem. Even if we hadn't encountered these unforeseen delays, the program was already about two months behind where it should have been. And this is not because we underestimated the program requirements. And it's also not because of lack of buy-in. People are truly optimistic about the ERP. Our Implementation Team is just not working as quickly as we had initially planned. It turns out that our 'Full Time Access' approach to resource capacity was not a smart one. Because over time, the resources from the Implementation Team have been pulled back more and more into their daily roles, which has left the ERP program on the backburner all too often.

When embarking on the ERP program, I knew that delays would be a constant threat to its success. I've seen it happen so many times in other companies, and I was determined not to let it happen to us. Of course, the Governance Committee is not happy with how far behind we are tracking, but nor am I. We are now around 6 months behind schedule, and I need to find a way not only to prevent further delays but also to lead us closer to the original deadline again. And just to add to this pressure, we've recently been approached by a competing consultancy with a merger proposal. This consultancy is large, internationally based, and has a strong presence in the Small to Medium-sized Enterprise (SME) market (an area that we've been eager to enter, if not for the risks involved). This merger would offer some obvious benefits, like increased market share, a less risky entry into the SME niche market, and the ability to build a pipeline of long-term clients by setting SME's up for growth, and then supporting them as they become larger clients. But we'll need to carefully consider this proposal before any final decisions are made. That in itself is going to be a monstrous task. But besides interrogating the other consultancy, we would also need to take a good look in the mirror. And right now the ERP program is not looking like our strong point. So, there's pressure to move this program forward quickly but without compromising on the effectiveness of the system. A tactical makeover is still not on the cards.

Dinika, Cecilia and I arrange a meeting to discuss a strategy for mobilizing dedicated resources on the ERP program. Dinika's first suggestion is to outsource assistance. "I understand why you would suggest that," I say to her. "But outsourcing is risky. I know this because we see the evidence every time we advertise a new job opening. We already have the best of the best. Anyone else is a runner up. And we can't have runners up working on our client engagement projects, or the ERP". Cecilia agrees. "You know, Isabella," she says, staring at her pen as she thinks, "we could still outsource help if we were strategic about where we place it." She's got my attention. "If we prioritized the primary job tasks and ERP tasks of each Implementation Team member according to task complexity and impact, then we could outsource the lowest ranking tasks. For example, we can't outsource data cleansing or testing, but we could potentially outsource some lower level day to day activities". Dinika and I like Cecilia's thinking. We agree on a course of action. Dinika and Cecilia will initiate this task ranking system so that we can start contracting help to take some of the load off of our Implementation Team. We'll do the same for any other staff members who are not currently assigned to the ERP but would be of more value on the ERP than in their current roles. We can then outsource temporary replacements for their regular responsibilities. I agree to raise this additional cost to the Governance team by emphasizing the cost and time savings in the long term, especially with merger discussions underway.

"Okay, more help is obviously a step in the right direction," I say, "but I don't think that it's enough of a step. Because what I'm seeing is a daily prioritization of core roles, over ERP responsibilities. What we need is an attitude shift". Cecilia agrees and notes that daily stand up meetings doesn't seem to be presenting enough news of progress. "Many of the team report on 90% "stucks" and 10% wins. And sure, most of the time the 'stucks' are attributed to capacity constraints. But I have definitely gotten the impression that they still don't get as much of a kick out of achieving their ERP-related goals as they do from achieving their day job priorities". As soon as Cecilia says these last few words, it all clicks. And it's so obvious! We've failed to do one essential thing in order to make the ERP program of high importance to the Implementation Team. We haven't built their responsibilities into their job descriptions or performance measures. Their superiors are conducting performance reviews, holding weekly meetings, setting performance measures, all based on their job descriptions and the everyday projects that they're working on. So who can really blame them for prioritizing their primary responsibilities? "The problem is that their direct superiors are not always close enough to the details of the ERP program," adds Dinika. After another hour of massaging this idea, we agree that we need to have the job description of each and every Implementation Team member adjusted to include ERP tasks. After all, these tasks will be applicable for another year at least. We'll also chat with their superiors about a split performance review process. We'll suggest that no more than 70% of Implementation Team member performance is measured according to their primary roles, and is measured and reviewed by their superior. The other 30%-plus will be measured and reviewed by their Team Lead, or, for those who *are* team leads, their performance will be reviewed by Cecilia. High performance will be incentivized by relevant rewards, like time-off after the timely completion of an ERP program milestone.

Happy with the practical outcomes, I excuse myself from the meeting. Rick and I have a dinner planned tonight, just the two of us.

Chapter 14: Managing Organizational Paralysis

I just hate it when the week kicks off with a bad Monday! Maybe it was the rainy weather, or maybe it was the broken coffee machine in the staff dining room. Either way, an 8am meeting with Scott Rogers has left me feeling annoyed and grumpy. It doesn't matter what logic we throw his way, what kind of approach we take, or who we involve, Scott is just not buying into the cloud-based solution that we've selected for the ERP. We're just not getting through to him. I wish he would accept that the solution has already been selected, and we're already well into its implementation. There's no turning back now, so we need to just move forward. Besides, I still firmly believe that we've made the right decision. But unfortunately, like it or not, I know that Scott has enough influence over his team to negatively impact their attitudes with his own skewed views. We've already seen that those reporting to him on the Implementation Team are working slower than others, and we've had to revisit a number of IT tasks that were incorrectly or poorly done. We're wasting time, and it's time we don't have. I've vented my frustration on this matter to Bob once before, and he hinted towards the unfortunate reality that we may need to consider letting Scott go. Bob's view is that he's too much of an obstacle and a delay and consumes too much of my energy across a number of projects. "This is not the first time you've had trouble with Scott, Isabella," he said to me last week, quite firmly. There's a pattern of immature, and frankly damaging, behavior from Scott. You've tried your darndest to change that pattern with logic, negotiation, and understanding. Now, it's time to get rid of him." Maybe he's right. But *firing* him? I don't know.

I'll give it more thought. But I have other, more pressing challenges to think about right now. And all of them are related to this merger. It's adding so much additional pressure on the

ERP implementation, and the delays are reflecting on us in a bad way. The team is exhausted, even with the help of a few outsourced support functions. I mean, this ERP program has been going on for nearly a year already, and we've still got a long road ahead of us. Our Implementation Team is feeling burnt out, demotivated, and frustrated with the overwhelming number of changes the merger is requiring. In fact, the whole firm is feeling exhausted.

The SPMO has been working hard to integrate the two firms in such a way that the value analyzed and predicted by our financial and governance experts actually materializes. Together, we've set up a merger portfolio for evaluating, selecting, prioritizing and authorizing tasks, allocations and other key decisions. The major programs encompassed in this portfolio include Brand Deployment, Business Process Reengineering, Network Refurbishment and Deployment, IT Systems Migration (including the ERP), Compliance, Team Integration and Structuring, and Cultural Integration. We have conducted all of the material, financial, legal and strategic due diligence, and were confident that we would be a strong fit. With the merging firm's experience and presence in the SME market, and our firm's capabilities in the corporate sector, the marriage was bound to bring about positive strategic growth. And I still believe that. But what we seem to have overlooked were the people. Each of the two firms has succeeded in their own rights because of their unique organizational cultures. We are different in how we plan, how we work, and how we communicate and interact. So with insufficient planning and foresight, the cultural fit has been filled with conflict, confusion, and disagreement. From formal systems and processes to casual workplace habits, our staff has not taken well to their new colleagues' ways of doing things. Further to this, planning the new management structures, and actually implementing them, has been nothing short of impossible. We've endeavored as far as we could to cascade the changes that come with the merger. By using an adaptive and phase approach for implementation, holding regular team building workshops and information sessions, and opening various Q&A forums to the staff, we had expected a more seamless merger. I can't help but think that this would all have been a lot easier if the timing didn't overlap with the ERP program.

With some seriously hard work from myself, Dinika and Cecilia, we've managed to bring the ERP program timeline closer to the initial 18-month forecast. It's now sitting at 20 months, thanks to the revised approach for resource allocation and capacity planning. But, the cost is now well over budget, estimated at close to a 25% increase over the original budget. This is largely due to delays, scope creep, issues with requirements management, and the earlier mismanagement of resources. Of course, Bob and the Governance Committee are pretty upset about the increased cost. But honestly, I am so tired of Bob coming down on me for all the problems but being unavailable to help me solve them before they become failures. He's so wrapped up in this merger that he's giving little attention to the ERP program unless it's to criticize. He's even called off our last three catch-up meetings because he was "too busy." How am I supposed to keep the ERP team motivated and energized when I don't even feel that way myself? And just to top it all off, we've been hearing rumors that some of our key talents are considering leaving the firm.

Arrrgh! I need a break. I tell Callie that I won't be in tomorrow, and ask her to move any meetings I have over to the second half of the week. Luckily, I have a nice and long drive planned – to visit my mom and dad with Rick and the kids. I heard my sister, Christina, is going to take the day off too and spend it with us. I think I will join them. It's strange, actually. Not too long ago, James and I were laughing at a social media post where a woman was praising her boss for encouraging 'mental health' days - just like sick leave for the mind. We thought it sounded quite ridiculous; an excuse to miss work, really. But I am *actually* starting to see the value in it. I feel like I'm on the edge of crazy, and so is the rest of the firm.

As I pull up to my parent's driveway the next afternoon, I see my sister's white Audi. She must have arrived early. I can hear her high pitched laugh the moment I open my car door. She's a high-energy, bubbly personality, and sometimes I find that draining. But today I'm looking forward to having some positivity and laughter in my space. "Sis!" she shouts with excitement as I walk into the kitchen where she's sitting with Mom and Dad. She gets up to give me a long hug. I greet my Mom and Dad with a kiss and eagerly accept a cup of hot coffee. Having not seen my sister for a few months, there's a lot to catch up on. Christina is in real estate. She's Head of Training for the residential property division of a reputable, U.S.-wide company. Sometimes I think her life sounds so easy. She travels around the U.S. training teams and then moving on. She's not responsible for motivating those teams to perform, she doesn't have to deal with their personal issues, and she certainly doesn't have to fire anyone on those teams. And to make it even easier, she has no husband and children to worry about.

We decide to take Mom and Dad out for lunch. It's a quaint little restaurant that runs out of an old barn which the kids like. We sit in the open courtyard under the shady trees, and I'm starting to feel more relaxed. Mom and Dad are doing very well regarding their health, and say that the doctor is very impressed with Mom's quick recovery. "He says I'm in good shape for my age, you know?" she tells us proudly. Dad just grins. "Mmm, you better watch out Dad," I say, being silly. "Looks like the Doc has a thing for Mom." We all laugh, except for my darling, sweet Mother whose embarrassment turns her cheeks to a rosy red color. After a delicious home-cooking style lunch, followed by tea, Mom and Dad take a walk through the restaurant's gardens with Rick and their grandkids. Christina and I get talking, and she tells me that she's actually been quite down lately. She says that she's feeling stuck. "I really don't know what it is, Issy," she says, looking down at the table. I'm just so… unfulfilled. "What do you mean? I ask with concern? "You've got a great job, you've done very well for yourself, and you're young and healthy." "I know Issy, I know. And I also know that I should be grateful for these things. But you see, every day I wake up, and I do the same thing. I train the same sorts of people, across the same American cities, on much the same training materials. Then I go home to be alone because I have nobody (well, other than Solly, of course)." Solly is her sausage dog. "And all my friends are too busy for me these days," she continues. "They've got husbands and babies to look after. So I find myself, bored, lonely even." By now I'm feeling terrible for her. She always seems so happy, so carefree, that I had just assumed her life to be, well, nicer than my own. But I'm starting to realize that, while the grass can be greener, it can also be shorter, harder, or less fertile. I'm starting to realize that my own problems, like balancing a career and family, might be someone else's desire. And I should probably be more content. I am also worried about my poor sister now. She doesn't want Mom and Dad to know, so I promise to keep it between us. But in return, I make her promise that we'll phone each other more often, and will arrange to meet up for lunch everything she is nearby. "Deal," she says with a big smile. "Thank you, Issy."

Feeling more refreshed than I ever expected, I return to the office on Wednesday determined to give the firm the same opportunity to rest. It's bold, but I'm going to propose that the firm shuts down for one day. In about three months, there's going to be a public holiday that falls on a Thursday. So in order to allow the ERP Implementation Team to relax over a long weekend, as well as the rest of the company, I want to recommend that we close for the day and all non-essential employees take the day off. We still have enough time to warn our clients and partners that we'll be closed, and we can use this reward to incentivize hard work toward meeting realistic ERP implementation and merger milestones. Closing down the whole firm is the only way to ensure that nobody works on their leave or answers 'urgent' emails and phone calls from colleagues at the office. It's the only way to force everyone to switch off for a while and rest. I suspect that our staff will take this "mental health" day as a sign of appreciation, a gesture that demonstrates that we care about them as people, with families and lives outside of the workplace.

But I don't believe that a day off is enough on its own to fix the cultural problems we're experiencing with the merger. So, I'm also going to propose that on the first day back after that same long weekend, we hold firm-wide workshops where the staff is divided into cross-functional groups of employees to discuss the biggest challenges they are experiencing in the merger. The key challenges or patterns that emerge from those workshops will then be passed on to the SPMO for consideration. An open floor for staff to voice their concerns, their frustrations, and their suggestions about how this merger could be smoother and easier for everyone. The purpose will also be to unite the firm as one large team that understands each other's problems across functions and departments and then works together to solve them. By limiting these workshops to our firm's staff (and excluding the merging firm), I think we'll be providing our staff with a safe place to feel heard and understood. This might just be the way to finally get their buy-in. Anyway, the semi-annual portfolio review meeting is taking place next week, so I'll soon know what the rest of our leadership thinks about my idea. Right now, though, I've got a meeting with Terrance. He's coming to the office for a mentor session. It has been seriously difficult to remain a committed mentor to Terrance over the past few months. I'm just so tired and struggling to maintain a balance between career, family, social and health. In fact, social was booted off the priority list some time back already. I've thought about finding a way out of my mentorship responsibilities many times already. To be fair to myself, Terrance did manage to successfully complete his project, with only a little help from me. His team won first place in the class. So I feel that I've made good on my promise. But, I also know that he still values my advice as he enters the working world of project management, and I happen to value the learning I derive from every meeting and phone conversations we have, too. It's strange, but advising Terrance and working through problems with him always seems to give me just a little more insight into my own problems.

By the end of the day, I'm exhausted all over again. But it wasn't all bad. My meeting with Terrance went well. With the help of Patricia Johnson, a new friend he made while working on the foodbank project, Terrance found an interesting position as a project coordinator in a marketing company working on animations. He's still finding his feet but enjoying the challenge while he does. I can tell that he's already eager to upskill himself further. So I've suggested that he complete the Project Management Institute's (PMI) CAPM certification, and then when he has more experience, to tackle the PMP certification. He sounded excited about progressing through the PMI certifications as he grows in his career. I did, however, also recommended that he give himself time to focus on the new job before jumping into another commitment. He says that his supervisor has been very supportive, but that he's already dealing with some major obstacles in his first project, including the resignation of one of their lead animators. The funny thing is, I'm dealing with a similar issue but on a much larger scale.

This morning I was informed that Scott Rogers has handed in his resignation, and he will be moving over to a competing firm. Honestly, this news came as a relief. Sure, it's sad to see someone with so much potential leave the firm. And we're going to need to replace him urgently so that he doesn't leave a gap in the ERP Implementation Team. But I'm only too happy to let someone else deal with Scott's resistance to change and disregard others' opinions. His ability to provide value is always going to be stunted by his character flaws unless he recognizes his own development areas. I actually think he was taken aback when we didn't counter offer in an effort to retain him. I had tried repeatedly to *coach him*.

Anyway, that's not the full extent of my problem. The real challenge is that Scott's not the only one leaving. We're starting to see a pattern in Executive Committee members resigning for opportunities outside of our firm. Of course, they're not all going over to the competition. Some are starting their own companies, others are using the opportunity to change the direction of their career, and one or two are even retiring. But whatever the reason, a mass exodus in the leadership team of the firm is going to reflect badly on our stability and growth. There's risk of staff fearing for their jobs, clients choosing a (seemingly) more secure service provider, and business partners becoming concerned about the stability of our relationship. Not to mention what the merging firm must think. If our leadership doesn't appear to believe in our future, or able to handle the increased pressure brought on by the merger and the ERP implementation, then how can the rest of the staff? I chatted with Professor Woo, and he advised that we do two things - urgently. The first is to investigate why executive members are leaving. That's not a problem. We have information from the exit interviews to use there. The second is to reassure our staff at every level that we are strong, that we are stable, and that there is nothing but growth in our future (in other words, no-one is losing their job). Unfortunately, the second one isn't going to be easy to do.

We're experiencing some delays on the regulatory clearance around the merger, and there's further difficulty in reconciling the firms' risk appetites and governance structures. So convincing staff that "all is well" is going to require clear, transparent, and repetitive firm-wide communication. We'll have to be honest about the obstacles, but follow that honesty with clear explanations of how we plan to overcome those obstacles. Professor Woo also suggested that, while we should disclose as much as we can to all teams, we should make an effort to highlight 'wins.' "Make a big deal about the merger milestones that are successful, and reward the staff for it," he said. "That's how you'll encourage more positive behavior and make them feel like they're part of something that's actually working." A good example of this has been the integration of our knowledge management systems and processes. Thank goodness for the KMP. It's saved us a lot of time. Apart from the adoption issues early on, we also ran into a contractual licensing issue with the content. But with everything now sorted, the KMP has been a big help with the merger and the ERP program.

Ah, the ERP program. Another pain in my side. How did something that was supposed to be so exciting become something so damaging to our firm's morale? With changes to project scope and timelines and the introduction of outsourced staff, we're starting to see an obvious decline in energy around the program. There's now a serious risk of the ERP becoming tactical, or worse, failing altogether. The merger is revealing some added complication, too, because the other firm uses an older, on-premise ERP system that's near the end of its life. The system is largely incompatible with our new system under construction, but we know it will be important to somehow "stitch" them together. Some of the others on the SPMO have suggested that we pause on the ERP implementation until we've sorted out the regulatory concerns on the merger and develop a roadmap for the two systems to work together. I've fought against this idea. I fear that pausing now will make it all the more difficult to pick up this program later on. Also, the other company's ERP system is outdated, and they know it. In the early discussions, they expressed both support and optimism of our cloud-based ERP system selection and thought they may adopt it as a part of the integration. Moreover, what I really want to see is the ERP Transformation becoming a portfolio of its own, a center of excellence. Well, I'm working on it. But in the meantime, we'll just have to manage the challenges carefully, with strong leadership and a clear intention to keep the firm strategically aligned and motivated. At least that's what I've tried to tell Bob. He's starting to question whether the tactical implementation is actually an option! Can you believe it? Would Dinika believe it? No. We're not taking any shortcuts, or applying lipstick to a Tier I system that we know has shortcomings. Well, not if I can help it. I'd rather abandon the program altogether than create a hybrid hodgepodge.

Should we abandon the program altogether?

Chapter 16: Balancing Life, Work, and More Work

Oh darn it, I'm late. Not today, I can't be late today. I've got to be at the Semi-Annual Portfolio Review meeting in half an hour. "Here Hun," says Rick as he hands me my briefcase and a flask of coffee. I pause in my flurry to smile and give him a quick kiss goodbye. "Go get 'em Sweetheart!" he shouts after me as I dart out the front door. Thank heavens for that man!

Fortunately its school holidays, so the traffic is a little better than usual. I make it with about 2 minutes to spare. "Morning Isabella," says Callie with a worried look on her face as I rush into my office and put my bag down. "Hi Cal," I say, slightly out of breath. "They're all in the meeting room. And I think they've started already", she says, nervously. "That's okay Cal, I'll catch up." I can see that Callie is anxious for me. She's one of the most observant people I've known. So while I haven't discussed the details of my troubles on the merger and acquisition, I know that she knows what's at stake and that I'm fighting a bit of a lone battle on some fronts. I quickly neaten my hair and jacket and walk calmly over to the meeting room. Callie was right, they *have* started already. But they don't seem to have gotten very far. Besides, I've more than acquainted myself with the agenda items, so getting up to speed shouldn't be a problem.

The first item is the ERP program. They're reviewing the program progress for the current year. As I walk in, Dinika is explaining that "The ERP is still in progress with a few bumps and bruises, but we've managed to overcome the major challenges..." "Ah, Isabella!" Bob interrupts. "Please sit down. We've just started. Dinika was updating us on the ERP". After I take my seat and greet everyone, Dinika asks if I'd like to pick up where she left off. "Well," I say, "we've tackled some significant firestorms on this program, and we've learned some major lessons too. The program has been long, it's been demanding on our resources, and integrating the system with that of the merging firm prior to our own implementation being complete has been an incredible challenge. The KMP has been a great help". "But we've had some issues on that, Isabella, haven't we?" asks someone. "Well, yes," I reply. "We initially had trouble getting staff to adopt the new knowledge management systems and processes, and then we encountered a licensing issue with the content. But we've managed to overcome both of those problems, and the KMP has since saved us a lot of time in the ERP implementation. We've also achieved a smooth integration of knowledge management processes in the merger. So, things are not perfect, but they're under control". I see a few nodding their heads in agreement.

"Our biggest problem today, in *my* opinion, is that we're experiencing severe organizational stress around resources and intellectual capital. Our staff is leaving, from the top down. We need to control those losses. I am also concerned about firm-wide support on the ERP and merger. We need strong organizational change management, together with strong leadership, to get our firm through the many changes underway. But currently, I feel that we, as the leadership, are not aligned with our views on the transformational objectives of the ERP program. The intention was for this to be a deep, strategic initiative. But lately there have been rumors of a more tactical approach, or even pausing, or abandoning the program altogether. So we need to make a decision, and realign ourselves to drive that decision forward with a team of exhausted staff members".

I immediately hear a few comment under their breath, and I sense some defensiveness. But this tough issue had to be raised. Finally, the first person speaks up, and then the next, and the next. All of a sudden everyone in the room seems to be using this open door as an opportunity to voice their opinions. But in the various, conflicting comments flying around, it becomes obvious that I'm right. We are all misaligned. I can tell that Bob is trying to remain fairly neutral, and lays out the various options. Some make the case for a tactical approach, two are in favor of pausing the ERP program but resuming as a strategic transformational initiative once the merger has regulatory clearance, and one feels that we should abandon the program altogether (he happens to be one of the executive committee members who is rumored to be leaving the firm!). However, the majority are still in favor of moving ahead with a strategic ERP.

We discuss how crucial it is that everyone, even those not in favor of the decision, supports the ERP as a continuing strategic program. This applies both to the role of leadership in setting an example, but also the role of every supervisor in motivating and rewarding performance on the ERP tasks and milestones. So, we agree that the ERP program should be realigned to its own portfolio and Center of Excellence (COE) and decide that we'll bring Dinika on board as the internal COE ERP Portfolio Manager. I'm so relieved of this outcome. I'm confident that this realignment of purpose and support will have a big impact on renewing the team's motivation, and alleviating some of the pressure I'm under, too.

Having finally concluded on the approach to managing the ERP, we move onto the next major theme, the merger. I have a host of new concerns and ideas on this front, and the atmosphere is already somewhat heightened. But, once again, I must speak up. A few attendees are already commending each other for great progress on the merger. But I have a different view for three primary reasons. Firstly, the other firm doesn't have robust project-program-portfolio management like we do. Thus, the marriage of the disciplines, methods, tools, techniques, and processes between our firms has been challenging, to say the least. Secondly, our resources are already almost completely tapped out on the COE ERP portfolio. So, I'm really worried that the added drain on resources for the merger is pushing the firm overboard. And finally, (and I hate to put the executives on the spot again), I don't feel that the Executive Committee members, including Bob, are appreciative of all the hard work that the teams have invested in to get the merger this far already. It's felt a little like business as usual, and so I'm not seeing a willingness from our leadership team to bring additional resources on board.

"This has really left me stuck between a rock and hard place," I say. "Our resources are too few and too tired to deliver the performance we need on both the ERP implementation and the merger integration. And, the merging firm has proved relatively unhelpful in the integration process because despite their many resources, they are insufficiently trained, and in my opinion, undisciplined". "I don't know that they're that unhelpful, Isabella," says Bob. "Why do you say so?" I've just raised a number of negative points regarding the merger, so it's not surprising that the atmosphere is growing tense. But, *wanting* the merger to be successful, and actually *making* it successful, are two different things, and to make it successful, we'll need to recognize the problems, and fix them. The first step though is recognition. "Well," I say to Bob, and the rest of the table, "attending their PMO was an eye opener of note. In fact, I found it to be chaotic. We're experiencing firestorms on most integration fronts, including cultural clashes, different reporting structures, incompatible systems and poor migration.

Our one hundred day integration plan should have tangible results, hearing recommendations that by day 100 we commence an evaluation of "X" is ludicrous. Not to mention that we're trying to keep to strict timelines and budgets. And unfortunately, while the other firm's knowledge of our target niche market is invaluable, their resources, training, structures, and discipline are messy and disorganized. In order to properly manage stakeholder expectations, communication, and risk, I really believe that we'll need to start with getting our PMO's aligned in thinking, approach and application. Strategic business execution has got to run at that heart of everything we do, as a united firm", I say passionately. "We've got to start at the top." There's a short period of silence while a few scratch their heads or shuffle in their chairs. "Well then," Bob finally speaks up, "I propose that Isabella be appointed Head of the Integration Team."

I take a deep breath like I'm about to take a dive into yet another deep, black ocean. I know I have no choice but to accept Bob's proposal. Or do I? How do I balance all these activities: my family and relationship with Rick and kids, my "day job" of running the SPMO, and now this enormous opportunity of leading the Integration Team that will in all likelihood make or break my career? Ahhh... so many things to do with so little time... What should I do?

For More Information...

The purpose of iExperi Press, a division of PMO Advisory, is to publish and promote insightful books that describe, explain, clarify, educate, and make real the many concepts, practices, processes, tools, and techniques related to strategic business execution.

PMO Advisory LLC is a leading project management training and consultancy. As a PMI Global R.E.P., it is one of the few firms in the world offering a full spectrum of project management training across agile project-, traditional project-, program-, portfolio-, and risk management including boot camps for PMI-ACP, CAPM, PMP, PgMP, PfMP, and PMI-RMP. Perhaps more importantly, PMO Advisory has a unique set of missions as a socially responsible firm

Others books in publication on Amazon and Kindle include:
1. The Sensible Guide to Passing the PfMP Exam: Including 400 Practice Exam Questions
2. The Sensible Guide to a Career in Project Management in 2015
3. The Sensible Guide to a Career in Project Management in 2016

For more information about PMO Advisory, please visit us at www.pmoadvisory.com. We also hope to receive your feedback, so please register this book here where you ask questions or provide us with feedback: www.pmoadvisory.com/product-registration/.

_____

Made in the USA
Las Vegas, NV
09 February 2021